FROM DANTE TO JEANNE D'ARC

From
DANTE TO JEANNE D'ARC

Adventures
In Medieval Life and Letters

BY

KATHERINE BRÉGY, Litt.D.

KENNIKAT PRESS, INC./PORT WASHINGTON, N. Y.

To
Edith and Virginia
a "Modernist" and a "Medievalist"
with the Author's Love

The author's grateful acknowledgment goes to Dr. Michael Williams, editor of *The Commonweal,* in whose pages the title-paper of this volume was published as a Prize Essay in 1927, and to John S. Leahy, Esq., of St. Louis, donor of the Thousand-Dollar Prize; to the Reverend James M. Gillis, C.S.P., editor of *The Catholic World,* in which magazine many of these studies originally appeared; and to the Funk and Wagnalls Company, for permission to reprint parts of an article contributed to the *International Book Review.*

PREFACE BY THE GENERAL EDITOR

The revival of interest in medieval literature and art, and the renewed appreciation of what was best and noblest in the life and institutions of the Middle Ages, have been among the most hopeful signs of our day.

Brilliant enthusiasts like Pugin in architecture, Ruskin in painting, Rossetti in poetry, and Walter Scott in the historical novel, turned back men's gaze to the riches of an earlier age. But little could even these leaders have anticipated the full trend of the movement they were helping to initiate in their own country and which at the same time was taking place in other lands. The great result was that by degrees the scales began to fall from the eyes of men and they were able to see with clearer vision the beauty and the wonder which for generations had lain hidden from their forbears.

With this transformation wrought, men might again look upward and behold with due appreciation the majesty and spiritual grandeur of the Gothic they had long been taught to ignore or to despise. The painting of the early masters once more claimed their attention and the frescoes of a Fra Angelico became a euphrasy for eager eyes. The stately measure of the stern and silent Florentine found ampler echo within countless souls and the great cantos of his mighty song became familiar in every tongue. Men followed him from nether Hell, up through the Purgatorial ways, and worshiped with veiled vision before the Mystery of the Triune God. "The eternal synthesis of Medievalism," Dr. Ralph Adams Cram has called Dante.

For scholar, artist, and historian the rediscovery of the Middle Ages, with all their preciousness of lore and learning and of human skill, was like the sighting of a new-found Ind or Tharsis, luring constantly more searchers in quest of undreamed riches and inspiring poets to sing the legends of the Table Round, the mystic glories of the Holy Grail, the argent stainlessness of Galahad, and the still more spiritual purity of the holy nun, the first to see again the sacred Cup, "rose-red, with beatings in it, as if alive." What wealth! What symbolism!

And yet, as we well know, not all was fair and glorious in those stirring days of the great Middle Ages. Men and women, then as now, were both intensely human, and often in their lives the good and evil strangely mingled. Even the rich romances of their poets not seldom needed to be looked upon with careful caution by a Church that is the Mystic Bride of Christ, begotten, as the Fathers beautifully taught, from His wide-opened side on Calvary. But whatever the lives of men might be, for better or for worse, they never lost sight of the great truths or hopelessly failed to distinguish good from evil, right from wrong.

The poetry and life of those once long-forgotten ages, are here revived for us. In the author's book, as in a mystic mirror of Shalott, we catch once more reflections of the lights and shadows, as they pass across the far-off scenes. We see the men and women, noble knights and fairest ladies, with all the pageantry and passion of their day, until we come to the close of all: the fierce, red, sunset glare of burning faggots, out of which soars upward — pure, indomitable and sublime — the heroic soul of Jeanne d'Arc. It is indeed "the sunset of the Middle Ages."

The author, whether as lecturer or writer, has made her own the wide field of literature, and within it particularly the one fair demesne of poetry, as witness her works: *The Poets' Chantry* and *Poets and Pilgrims,* both written in a rich vein of sympathetic appreciation, while *Bridges* is her own distinctive tribute to the Muses.

Miss Brégy, in her early girlhood, was favored by the advice and friendship of Alice and Wilfrid Meynell, and her poetry during subsequent years made its welcome appearance in leading reviews. Her devotion to French culture, as a descendant of the literary Comtesse Charlotte de Brégy or Brégi and daughter of the late Judge Amédée Brégy, of Philadelphia, merited for her two decorations bestowed by the French Government. In the present instance her combined scholarship and artistry have risen to the opportunity afforded her in this series of medieval studies, introduced by her widely known Dante essay, which won the international Leahy prize offered by the *Commonweal* and now makes its first appearance between the covers of a book.

JOSEPH HUSSLEIN, S.J., PH.D.,
General Editor, Science and Culture Series

St. Louis University

CONTENTS

[xiii]

DANTE'S DREAM OF LIFE*

M Y FRIEND, but not the friend of fortune" — that
is the description of Dante which he puts upon
the lips of the blessed Beatrice when, at the opening of the
Divine Comedy, she summons Virgil to rescue her poet from
the "dark wood" of his wanderings. So, apparently, in his
riches and his poverty, he liked best to think of himself: and
after six hundred years there seems no better way for us to
think of him. Stranger and pilgrim upon earth, a tragic
comedian he must remain to the common-sensible man — but
friend immortally of the woman who had been his revelation first of human love, and then of divine Wisdom.

Dante Alighieri lived in what Wilde has aptly called
"symbolic relations" with his own age: and it was, of course,
one of the most stormy and most stimulating in human
history. He had the good fortune to be born in the second
half of the thirteenth century — very arch of the bridge of
Medievalism which stretched, by way of the Dark Ages,
back to the old order of dubious, glorious Antiquity; by way
of the Renaissance, on to the paradoxes of our glorious,

*This paper — originally entitled *Dante and His Vision of Life* — won, in
1927, the Leahy Prize of one thousand dollars offered in international competi-
tion, through the *Commonweal* magazine, for the best essay on Dante.

dubious Modernity. When, in the May of 1265, he was born at Florence, Italy was in the midst of her long Guelf and Ghibeline warfare. Manfred as hope of the waning Empire and Urban IV as that of the Papacy, faced each other; while Charles of Anjou had arrived in Italy to settle these perpetual feuds as the French Pope naturally thought they ought to be settled. It happened that his coming did establish the supremacy of the Guelf party, to which Dante's father belonged, in Tuscany. But the bitter Black and White controversies were still ahead, so that anything called peace in thirteenth-century Florence was merely in the nature of a breathing space.

Yet if Italy — in fact, the whole seething world of Europe — knew little external peace, it knew marvelous creative energy in every field and had an amazing interest in politics, philosophy, theology, and a few other sciences and arts. It was a time of high-lights and heavy shadows. Francis of Assisi and St. Dominic were less than half a century dead when Dante was born. Aquinas, the Angelic Doctor, and Bonaventura, the Seraphic Doctor, were still living; so were Roger Bacon and Albertus Magnus, grown already old, while Duns Scotus and Meister Eckhart were almost as young as our poet. St. Louis reigned in France, although his life and the Christian hope in the East were soon to be sacrificed in the desperate hope of the last Crusade.

All over Christendom legal forms were becoming settled, and chivalric grace was tempering the force of feudalism. The universities of Bologna and Oxford were thriving, while that of Paris, a century after Abélard, must have seemed already venerable. And everywhere men and women, too, rejoiced in poetry, in romance. The vernacular was emerging, daring to lift its young, sweet voice in songs

of troubadour and minnesinger, in the love poems of Italy
and the prayer poems of England. Mystery cycle and miracle
play rubbed shoulders with the Arthurian legend and the
naïve sophistication of Aucassin and Nicolette or the
Romaunt of the Rose. And wherever the Gothic inspiration
had lifted up men's souls and hands, they were already
fashioning a Europe "new washed to its irradiant birth"
in the sister arts. One does not, perhaps, like to remember
that of our familiar Florence Dante can have known only
an unfinished Baptistery and the beginnings of Santa Maria
Novella, Santa Croce and the Palazzo Vecchio. But in Paris
he must have seen Notre Dame in her mysterious youth
and the newly completed radiance of the Sainte Chapelle.

Among his own Florentine contemporaries, Cimabue
and Giotto were a little older — Boccaccio, Villani, and
Petrarch a little younger. As a boy, Dante seems to have
been rather a favorite protégé of the learned Brunetto Latini;
and since his family was only distantly noble and not
conspicuously wealthy, this intimacy and the subsequent
one with the young Prince Carlo Martello have been cited
to show that he was already proving himself a youth of
"parts." But about his actual schooling in those early years
we know practically nothing. It is evident from references
throughout his works and from his later civic activities, that
Dante had — like so many sons of the Renaissance — con-
siderable knowledge of design and architecture. And the
author of the *Vita Nuova* was emphatically not ignorant
of the Seven Liberal Arts. But through that whole early
work the young scholar is carefully obscured by the young
lover. So is the young soldier, although we know that
Dante saw active military service and probably fought at
the battle of Compaldino. But he was writing subjectively,

[3]

impressionistically even — and only of the things which mattered vitally in the development of his love life. The first glimpse of little Beatrice Portinari in her dress of "subdued and goodly crimson" mattered overwhelmingly; so did the year 1290 when "the Lord God of Justice called that most gracious Lady to Himself." Yet Dante never thought it worth while to mention her marriage to Simone Bardi, nor his own subsequent espousal of Gemma Donati. And probably, in the spacious perspective of the soul and the centuries, he was quite right.

However intensive his self-teaching, Dante could scarcely have become one of the greatest scholars of his scholarly age without study at some of the great contemporary universities. So, as we know he did attend both Paris and Bologna, it seems likely that his first sojourns there may have been after Beatrice's death; when, as the *Convito* tells us, he turned for consolation to Wisdom, seeking her "in the schools of men of religion and at the discussions of philosophers" — before the political activities which date from about his own thirtieth year.

Young Alighieri's love for Florence was an intense and impassioned thing, like his love for justice: indeed, like all his loves and hates. As soon as his voice began to be heard in the councils of the city, it was raised invariably and fearlessly against the outside interference and outside levies which, under whatever provocation, ended always in the bloodshed so common in medieval communities or the graft so common in our own. It was a curious irony that he should have been elected to office of prior in that very year 1300 when Pope Boniface VIII, at the instance of the Black faction of Florentines, once again tried the experiment of asking a French prince to intervene as peacemaker. This time it was Charles

of Valois, whom Dante bitterly opposed — but history repeated itself. And as the earlier French invasion had spelt
the prosperity of his childhood, so this latter spelt the temporal ruin of his maturity: his disgusted veering away from
the Guelf and toward the Ghibeline party, his lifelong en-
mity against Boniface and all papal activity in politics, and
immediate exile from his native city. It seems to have been
in 1302 or 1303 that Dante turned his face from Florence,
never to return. For to the original sentence of banishment
with confiscation of his goods, a decree of death was later
added.

Then for twenty years he was to learn

> how salt his food who fares
> Upon another's bread — how steep his path
> Who treadeth up and down another's stairs . . .

He studied prodigiously, probably at Bologna and Paris
again, possibly even farther north; and Scartazzini's supposition* that he also taught at these and other schools seems
most credible. The disenchanted exile had only learning to
commend him at Lucca, or at Can Grande's court in Verona;
or at Ravenna, where he died shortly after completing a diplomatic mission for Guido da Polenta in 1321. But what
really matters is that those years of wandering and heartache
bore fruit in one of the greatest masterpieces in all literature
— the *Comedy* men have agreed to call *Divine*.

Its inspiration had, of course, come long before: for if
Dante's wisdom were indeed the "child of suffering," his
beauty was the "child of love." All the world of romance
knows the story — for he has told it in that curious rhapsody,
the *Vita Nuova* — of how love came to him in the person of

---

*Scartazzini, *Companion to Dante*, Part II, Chap. 2.

[5]

the Florentine maiden, Beatrice Portinari. Everything about her took on immense and occult meaning, everything gave subject for sonnet or canzone. She was exquisite, she was unattainable, she came in vision and all untimely "hid her face amid a crowd of stars." And it might have been just like a thousand other romances in the chivalric convention — except that this happened to be a great and not a little passion. "When she appeared in any place, it seemed to me . . . there was no man mine enemy any longer," wrote the proud, tempestuous youth; "and such warmth of charity came upon me that most certainly in that moment I would have pardoned whosoever had done me an injury." But neither his own transcendentalism nor the trappings of romance can disguise how unsatisfactory he must have seemed to the lady herself, in his dizzy, inarticulate adoration — or worse still, in the mad ingenuity of choosing another lady for "screen" and addressing verses to *her!* The most human thing Dante ever tells us of Beatrice — more human even than the tears shed for her father's death — was her refusal to greet him when gossip of that little vicarious flirtation was particularly rife. But he only wondered, and went home, crushed, to write more verses about it all. At last even he saw the folly of these concealments, and in spite of the popular convention of secrecy, openly proclaimed his devotion, so that because of his songs and her own exceeding loveliness Beatrice became the legend of Florence: "When she passed anywhere folk ran to behold her. . . . She went along crowned and clothed with humility, showing no whit of pride in all that she heard and saw; and when she had gone by, it was said of many 'This is not a woman, but one of the beautiful angels of Heaven.' " Already she embodied all the virtues he himself needed most — meekness, magnanimity, that "peace" which he calls else-

where the "crown of every good." And when, musing one day
"how frail a thing life is though health keep with it," he is
rapt into sudden prophetic vision of her own leavetaking,
his prayer to Death is simply: "Now come unto me, and be
not bitter against me any longer; surely there, where thou
hast been, thou has learned gentleness. . . ." But it was only
to Beatrice that Death came in the June of 1290, leaving Florence "widowed and desolate" like Jerusalem of old. For a
while Dante continued to pour his immense grief into the
mould of his little verses, driving himself to illness and naturally attracting a good deal of feminine sympathy. It matters little enough now whether the "Lady of the Window"
was (as he implies in the *Vita Nuova*) a very human person
of whom he thought temporarily "as of one too dear," or
(as he liked to believe in the later *Convito*) a symbol of
philosophy. Life, to the mystical temperament, has always
the dual meaning which he so constantly claims for his own
words — *real* and *allegorical*. And when he faces Beatrice
at the close of the *Purgatorio,* he confesses candidly enough
that there had been detours of sense and imagination, too —
treacheries for which he paid in bitter self-reproach. Perhaps
even these were necessary, that he might learn for all time
how dear was the ideal he had momentarily betrayed. But
Death lifted that fragile, unfulfilled romance up into Immortality, and in the mysterious nearness of Eternity, Beatrice
was to possess him beyond shadow of change or misunderstanding. Incentive and inspiration too, little by little the
Lady of his delight was transmuted into a symbol of all
truth, all grace, all wisdom, the very sum of God's revelation
to man. It was a milestone not only in Dante's life but in the
history of romantic love when that "wonderful vision" came
which determined him to "say nothing further of that most

blessed one" until he should be able to put into words "what hath not before been written of any woman." So the end of the *Vita Nuova* became the prelude to the *Divine Comedy*.

While many of the Dante legends, like many of the Dante letters, are, of course, dubious, it is quite possible from his own and other contemporary words to conjure up a picture of this apocalyptic figure: the young, eager boy, alternately studying, fighting, and writing mystical love poems; the man devoted to learning and civic righteousness, embittered by the injustice which drove him into exile; the proud, wandering scholar, a bowed figure, courteous yet "melancholy and thoughtful," as Boccaccio tells us, loving to live "apart from mankind, that his meditations might not be interrupted" — until in his fifty-seventh year Death found him, far from Florence, his "mother of little love." How important Dante had become almost immediately after his death Villani shows by the space devoted to him in his history of the city; adding that because of his learning (but we could divine other reasons!) he was "somewhat arrogant, fastidious, and disdainful."

Finally, Dante's own minor works complete the many-sided personality. Along with the *Vita Nuova* one remembers those early lyrics in the *"dolce stil nuova"* which would have ranked Dante high as a love poet if he had not himself superseded them. Very revealing, too, is the unfinished *Convito* or *Banquet,* in which he attempts to break the bread of knowledge to those who hunger. The book, probably begun in Florence and continued in exile, is a series of poems with long accompanying glosses on all sorts of subjects. Autobiography is touched upon, so are love and learning and the Nine Angelic Choirs! Its observations upon the vernacular —a subject naturally dear to Dante, since he was the first great poet daring enough to confide a masterpiece to it — anticipate his Latin treatise *De Vulgari Eloquentia*. And its glorification of the Roman Empire anticipates that most curious and intellectually obsolete of all his works, *De Monarchia*. It is easy enough for the modern mind to see in the "Holy" medieval Empire a mere survival of the antique order, bound to disintegrate before the developing nationalities of Christendom. But to contemporary imaginations this idea of a peaceful, universal dominion may well have loomed as some such panacea as the League of Nations seemed after our recent war. Dante apotheosized it as a haven of harmony in which man might be free to seek learning and God, an image of the undivided monarchy of Heaven, a government divinely established in the secular order as the Church was in the spiritual. His work, with its sometimes fanatical fulminations against any pope who ventured to regulate or dictate to this Empire, is sheer political propaganda, written in good faith but in all the heat of party prejudice. Yet in a poet bruised and weary from the warring of faction against faction, city against city, it is at least a comprehensible reaction.

The two things dearest to Dante on the human side — Beatrice and Florence — life took from him before he was thirty-eight years old, giving in their place "heart's hunger and soul's thirst, and blessedness beyond the pride of kings." It was the blessedness of creating a poem which should so perfectly concentrate all the knowledge and inspiration of his own age that it must forever teach and inspire the ages to follow. Obviously he could never have done this without the treasures of creative genius, profound learning, and rich if searing experience. Without his disillusion, his hatred of injustice, he could never have conceived the *Inferno;* without the falls and risings of his own *Via Crucis* he could not have dramatized the *Purgatorio;* without his yearning love for the Supreme Good, and for the human image of it he had found in one woman, he could scarcely have pictured that *Paradiso* which is simply the sublimation of Light and Love.

When he took for subject that arresting fifth act of man's pilgrimage which is played upon the stage of Eternity, Dante faced an audience whom poets and preachers had already made familiar with visions and other-world voyages, for whom the curtain between material and spiritual things constantly fluttered back and forth. He had the advantage of not having to argue any of his essentials: what he had to do was to build a cathedral where there already existed a wayside shrine. So he placed the Hell, in which all his contemporary readers believed, just where they believed it to be — in circles narrowing down to the center of the earth. Concerning its punishments he could give imagination free rein, within the simple limits of the Church's teaching. He could here be as concrete as he liked: and he never hesitated to speak as politician as well as poet and prophet.

But while many of Dante's passionate personalities have grown uninteresting or unintelligible with the centuries, we are as near as he to the "Trimmers" — choosers neither of good nor of evil upon earth — whom he assigns to a perpetuity of paltry pains just inside the gate of Hell. *Leave all hope, ye that enter here,* is the grim legend of that portal. . . . Very near it, in a merciful "sadness without torment," he places the Heathen and Unbaptized; and from this realm his "beloved father," Virgil, has come to be his guide through the Underworld. The first circle of absolute punishment is that of the Carnal Sinners; where men and women — for there is no "double standard" here — are tossed endlessly upon the winds of passion, and where Dante introduces the exquisite episode of his meeting with Francesca da Rimini. These are but the first of the sinners against *continence,* the others being the Gluttonous, the Avaricious, and the Wrathful. Below them looms the dread City of Dis, with the Heretics lying lonely in their burning tombs, and all the circles of increasingly malicious evil: the river of blood choking the Murderers and Tyrants, the pitiful wood of the Self-Destroyers, the rain of fire upon those who had sinned in violence against God or Art (Order) or Nature. For the most part, Dante's allegory is obvious enough, sometimes with grotesquerie as well as poetry in the punishments — the Evil Counselors floating like willful flames, the Sowers of Schism with their own bodies horribly and symbolically rent, the metamorphoses of the Thieves, suggesting Fafner's change into the dragon guarding his own gold. But under whatever allegory, it is distinctly terrible to be able to visualize so many souls — souls of his neighbors and friends as well as his enemies — in unending torment. Justice is a difficult virtue to handle, and Dante as *judge* alone, without love linking him to "man's unpardonable race," would scarcely have survived the ages. But in Purgatory he was to learn of a soul saved "by one little tear" — in Paradise to hear the warning, "We who see God know not as yet all the elect."

Constantly throughout this pageant of "terror and pity" one is struck by the innate refinement of Dante's thought. It was characteristic that only for the Simonists was his indignation greater than his compassion: to the other tormented souls he brings "not contempt but sorrow." His momentary curiosity to listen to the wrangling of fiends is rebuked by Virgil as a "vulgar wish" — and, perhaps, because he never finds them amusing, he can treat all the intricacies of evil with less than the candid coarseness of our robust and radiant Chaucer.

The atmosphere of Hell is essentially abnormal, but there is a very human touch in the punishment of familiar mortal diseases, without the familiar hope of recovery, meted out to the Falsifiers in Words and Deeds and Things. And persistent among these fallen ones Dante finds the inscrutable wish to be remembered. "So may your memory not fade from human minds" is the lure certain to win an answer from them. Certain, except in that innermost ninth circle where all is frozen, and the Traitors, with faces "made doggish by the cold," have slipped below the final fellowship of human motives. Here, confined in a central well of ice, is Satan the archtraitor — gigantic, three-headed, with bat wings keeping the intolerable winds astir. It is by no means a subtle Mephistopheles, for Dante seems to have spent none of his creative genius on this figure of ultimate evil. He was content with the typical fiend of medieval art — a fallen, frozen figure, the *negation* of all effective life and light and warmth and love.

On the other hand, there is a curious and comforting mixture of the human and the divine in his Mount of Purgatory, where penitent man consorts with sympathetic angels and may still learn from the beauties of Nature and of art. It is all familiar ground: for once the Ante-Purgatory is passed — where Negligent Rulers, the late Repentant and those who die suddenly while Excommunicate must wait before beginning their bittersweet ascent — Dante kneels before the angel of the doorway, most palpably representing Confession, and bidden to err "in opening rather than in keeping shut. . . ." Within, the first sound he hears is a surging *Te*

Deum Laudamus, for Purgatory is a place of joy and prayer as well as of pain — such joy as the woman has in her travail. Also it is a place of that *love* which one of the poet's most pregnant passages declares "the seed of every virtue and every deed deserving punishment." The sins atoned for here are the sad perennial seven of our daily lives — familiar enough in Hell also when *unrepented* — and sins every one of love defective, excessive, or perverted.

First comes the circle of the Proud, consoled by the Angel of Humility as they stagger under their burden of stones. Next above are the blind Envious, learning at last the joy of sharing all good; then the Wrathful, groping their way through deep and bitter fog. In the fourth circle the Slothful are goaded on; in the fifth the Avaricious and the Prodigal suffer, suggestively enough, for the same essential fault: and so the tale is told.

Everywhere Dante meets old friends or makes new ones, everywhere the shadow betraying his living body raises eager inquiry. And everywhere the longing for prayers — or for messages to their beloved left on earth — wins from the souls those confessions of which, in the *Inferno,* ambition had been the motive. Among the emaciated Gluttonous he encounters the gay companion of his youth, Forese Donati — but most of the young love poets are to be found in the highest circle of all, where the "last wound" of our sensual nature is purged in flame! Here are Guido Guinicelli and Arnault Daniel, who "weeps and goes a-singing," and even for joy of Dante's converse will not stir beyond the cleansing sea of fire. Presently the Angel of Purity prays Dante himself to plunge into the flames; and he recoils in horror until the faithful Virgil reminds him, "Twixt Beatrice and thee is this wall." Then he, too, leaps into the holy fire — and issuing from its purification, finds himself at the entrance of Eden, the Earthly Paradise lost by man's original sin. "Crowned now and mitered" over himself, he must take leave of Virgil, the wise poet chosen to represent human Reason; for further initiation will come from Beatrice, his symbol of divine Faith or Revelation.

She is waiting for him, when the colorful pageant of Faith has passed — precisely the sort of pageant Dante must have seen at many a medieval festa, only sublimated to the nth degree — but at the very threshold of Paradise he falls weak beneath the "mighty power of ancient love. . . ." He is weaker still when her rebuke brings the shamed confession of ancient infidelity, until pitiful angel hands plunge him into the waters of Lethe. But it is not enough that the evil of life be forgotten — its good must be recalled. So the *Purgatorio* ends as he is bathed yet again in the sister-stream Eunoe: then, with Beatrice for guide, he stands ready to climb the ladder of stars into Paradise.

One reason for Dante's consummate success throughout this supreme work is his balance of novelty and familiarity, of imagination and intellect; and nowhere is this balance more rigorously maintained than in the *Paradiso*. Scaling with sure step the peaks of sublimity, he does not forget that the purpose of the *Comedy,* as declared in his letter to Can Grande, is ethical rather than speculative. And just as his moral teaching avoids the noble but morbid reactions of untempered asceticism, so his devotion avoids, or rather controls, the excesses of untempered rapture. It is perhaps the crucial test of his integrity in art and life, too, that he is more intent upon the truth as he conceives it than even upon the inebriating beauty of his subject.

Doctrinally, of course, he builds upon the Scriptures and

the *Summa:* as setting he uses the admirably allegorical Ptolemaic system of astronomy. In his first initiation into the Paradisal vision, the souls are symbolically manifested in the "many mansions" of their Father's House — the ascent from circle to circle being revealed by the increasing beauty of Beatrice's face. In the Heaven of the Moon are the happy souls whose earthly stain was inconstancy — particularly to a solemn vow: but questioning whether this lower state of blessedness brings any lessening of joy, Dante receives the immortal answer, *E la sua voluntate e nostra pace.* That is the first and the last lesson Paradise has to teach — *In His will is our peace.* He finds it again in the Heaven of the Moon, which harbors those souls in whom human love too ardently contended with Love Divine: yet "Here we not repent but smile," since God is the eternal Lover and Artist, too, joying in each completed phase of His work. In the Heaven of the Prudent the singing, circling suns pause a moment while Thomas Aquinas rehearses the story of the Poverello — then, with reciprocal courtesy, Bonaventura comes to praise Dominic. In Mars of the Courageous, Dante confronts his ancestor Cacciaguido, who foretells his banishment and bids him never to conciliate men by tempering the truth of his vision. And as celestial gravitation draws them still upward, Dante is instructed by Beatrice and other saints upon difficult questions of faith, yet warned of truths never wholly to be compassed save by those whose wit is "matured within love's flame."

Individuality, personality even, is never lost: but definite and dazzling as the poet's imagery is, he lets us understand that *reality* still escapes. In the Seventh Heaven Beatrice does not smile nor the Blessed any longer sing lest Dante be shattered by excess of joy. More and more, as they pass the realm of the Fixed Stars, through the Primum Mobile and into the divine quiet of the Empyrean, the spectral colors are focused into one blaze of perfect light. Even Beatrice must leave him at last, returning to the mystical, luminous rose whose petals are the thrones of the saints. There is only Mary, joy of the angels, her face "most likened unto Christ's," who may obtain for him the Beatific Vision of God. It is granted. With sight miraculously unconsumed Dante reads

> In one volume clasped of love, whate'er
> The universe enfolds,

while by sudden, sublime intuition he apprehends the mysteries of the Trinity and the Divine and Human Nature. But from this ultimate revelation he comes stunned and silent, like every other authentic seer: *Eye hath not seen nor ear heard, nor hath it entered into the heart of man....* Only he knows that *peace* has come at last, and henceforth his will must roll onward like a mighty wheel,

> By the love impelled
> That moves the sun in Heaven and all the stars.

Writing in the "vulgar" tongue and choosing the familiar title of "Comedy," Dante seems to have set out deliberately to popularize the teaching of saint and philosopher and his own great dream. Yet no one could pretend that it is or ever was easy reading. Indeed, so profound are its disquisitions that in any language less incorrigibly musical than the Italian they could scarcely be claimed as poetry at all. His faith was highly intelligent, even highly intellectualized. There was hardly a doctrine of Catholic Christianity as defined in his day which Dante did not embody in his work: God the First Cause and Final End of Creation; our Redemption by Christ and its necessity; Free Will, Sin, and because of God's justice, Hell, Purgatory, and Heaven; the Church, with Prayer and Sacraments; the Virgin's power and loveliness — all these are the commonplaces (only never commonplace!) of his thought: so that Pope Benedict XV, magnanimously passing over Dante's personal animosity toward earlier prelates, could declare his work the very "juice of Christian philosophy and theology."*

But being a poet, and holding fast to what Patmore called the vital and mystical "corollaries" of belief, Dante bequeathed us not a catechism but a work of art. And who, in all the ages, has been more perfectly equipped to write the romance of the human soul in all the changes of the purgative, the unitive, and the illuminative ways? For Dante loved the *beauty of holiness,* and knew the price which in our bruised world must be paid for all beauty. Like our own contemporary Paul Claudel, the medieval Florentine had learned to fathom and to face a universe in which "Love has ended in pain, but pain has ended in love."

---

*Encyclical of His Holiness on the Dante Sexcentenary, 1921.

NOTE: Quotations from the *Divine Comedy* used throughout this paper are from the English version in the Temple Classics — except the last two in verse, which are Cary's: those from the *Vita Nuova* are, of course, D. G. Rossetti's.

WHEN ROMANCE MET RELIGION

THE term "romance" is of very variable significance nowadays — and indeed it can never have been easy of precise definition. It is rather too vast a thing for human computation; so our tendency is to belittle, to dismember it, or else to take refuge in a vague and sentimental use of the word. The thing itself is, without doubt, somewhat vague and sentimental; but our error is in attaching an unfavorable meaning to these terms. We speak with a certain contemptuous tolerance, a sense of fiction mistaken for fact, about the "romance of youth." And of late it has become fashionable to talk about the "romance of science" — most of us being respectful even if unconvinced when the stupendous achievements and possibilities of material science are in question. But there is still a suspicion of unreality and exaggeration about the word, and practical people are shy of mentioning the romance of labor, or the romance of religion, or the very essential romance of life. That is a thousand pities; that is where practical, modern people are both disappointing and impractical! Have we forgotten that romance is one of the most real and salutary facts in the universe — that it is necessary just because it seems so unnecessary? Romance is the glory of sunset and the glamour of purple mist; it is the wonder and tenderness of life; the essence of poetry; the seeking and finding of the ideal. And even the most practical of us cannot go very far without some sort of an ideal before or beside us.

Children infallibly love romance and move in a world of romantic creations, and there was a time when men and women did the same. They were not jaded or world-weary, and their heritage was one of robust physique, robust imagination, and robust faith. The outer life and the inner life were alike romantic to the medieval mind. Man was born into a world of conflict and mystery. On one side was the pride of life, the lust of the eyes and of the senses; varicolored garments and shining armor, song and wine and love and war. On the other was a haunting vision of

> Death waiting in his shoe,
> Him quietly to foredo —

a consciousness of sin; mighty penance; a very real and poignant yearning for the crucified Savior Knight or Ladye Mary, the Mother of might and gentleness. There was a terrible romance in the medieval thought of Hell, with its eleven grim and significant torments and its "loathly devil," to look upon whom man might well die of care! And there was just as sensible a romance — although some critics are less quick to recognize it — in the vision of Paradisal joys. Bernard of Cluny's *Jerusalem the Golden* — its radiant walls reëchoing "the shout of them that triumph, the song of them that feast" before their risen Prince — is a notable instance. But, of course, the most supreme testimony of all is found in the pages of Dante's *Divina Comedia*. No human mind has expressed the heights and depths of spiritual experience more transcendently, nor more romantically, than this medieval Florentine — whose visions have made real for all ages the glories of Heaven and the uttermost depths of Hell. But in case the testimony of this immortal poet and seer be considered unique, it is interesting to turn to humbler exemplars — for instance to the nameless bards of twelfth- and thirteenth-century England, where, in the welding of Norman and Anglo-Saxon elements, a new literature was coming to birth. We shall find upon every second page how blithely romance met religion — how naturally, and how fruitfully.

For in all this literature, there was as yet no conscious distinction between realist and romanticist; indeed, the realist *was* the romanticist. Nothing was so unromantic as to be just what it seemed, and there was no fact, objective or historical, which the medieval mind could not elucidate or at least analogize. The rainbow's blue, clearly, was an emblem of water, the first destroyer; its red symbolized fire. The habits of beast and bird, the properties of stone and mineral, had all some relation to man and the Maker of man. And this vigorous poetic quality — grotesque, sublime, whatsoever its accidental expression — was the fruit at once of *simplicity* and of *mysticism*. Simplicity — the childlike wish to be vivid, to picture a thought strikingly and astonishingly; and mysticism — that profound instinct of the medieval mind, that belief or intuition of the sacramental nature of human life.

And so we have the incidental romance of illustration and imagery. Unconscious, atmospheric as it was, it pervaded the entire literature of a period almost wholly religious in its written expression. Sermons, works of discipline or edification, were as picturesque as they were practical; and in the midst of some tense homily, we come upon one of those haunting and elemental bits of poetry, the debate of the Soul

and Body. More and more distinctly this union came to form
the warp and woof of the literary texture. To be sure, the
rule worked both ways; for while we find spiritual ideals
constantly blending with heroic in the secular epics, religious
lyrics were becoming as ardent and tender as love songs. The
whole medieval attitude toward life is wondrously revealed
if we but remember this — for always literature is in the
nature of a revelation.

Conventions and "types" there are, incontestably, in the
oldest of surviving romances; yet there has never been a more
faithful mirror of contemporary ideals. The immortal *Chan-
son de Roland,* while of French origin, came to England
with the Conqueror, and thereafter proved itself not only the
vigorous, esthetic delight of two nations, but preëminently
their code and inspiration. It is a very naïve romance, and
almost as religious as it is warlike. When the invincible Roland sinks, spent at last, upon the green grass of Roncevaux,
his thoughts — the minstrel tells us — are of "many things."
They are of "Sweet France," of the lands he has conquered,
of Charlemagne his lord, and the men of his race. . . . But
most poignantly of all they are of God. To Him Roland
proffers his gauntlet in token of homage, and striking his
breast, he begs forgiveness:

> *Dieu! c'est ma faute, pardon par ta puissance*
> *Pour mes péchés, les grands et les petits,*
> *Que j'ai commis dès l'heure où je suis né.*

There seems nothing inharmonious in the appearance of
Gabriel and those other bright spirits who bear the count's
soul away to Paradise — the scene is all so artless and so
natural in its supernaturalism. *"Ni l'antiquité n'avait inven-*

té, ni la poésie Chrétienne n'a su retrouver de pareils accents pour peindre une mort héroïque et sainte," comments M. Petit de Julleville.*

In the foregoing instance the romance was, of course, essential, and the religious element merely (if very vitally) interpenetrated. But the order was often reversed. Then, as always, the priest was contemporaneous. He who would save the soul of knight or serf, of lady or anchoress, had need to remember the ubiquitous romance; and he had need to incorporate into his own work something of its winsome and exciting quality. So here is the balladlike beginning of an early *Assompcioun de Notre Dame:*

> A merry tale tell I this day,
> Of Seinte Marye, that sweet may,
> All is the tale and high lesoun
> And of her sweet assompcioun . . .

While another pious versifier, with most engaging gentleness toward the weakness of the flesh, thus opens up his *Passional:*

> Hearken now this little tale that I to you will tell,
> As we find it written down in the holy Gospel;
> It is not of Charlemagne, nor of his twelve peer,
> But of the Lord Christ's sufferings that He endured here.

In the prolific field of legendary and apocryphal history, it is practically impossible to draw any hard-and-fast line between the romantic and religious elements. No group of writings seem to have been more universally popular. The

Histoire de la Littérature Française.

clergy approved because they were edifying, the people rejoiced because they were most indubitably interesting — and
so they flourished apace. Such was the exuberance of creative
imagination that before long the very stones of the Temple,
porch and column and roof and spire, were overgrown by
this tangled if flowery vine of fancy. There was a whole series
of legends concerning the Holy Rood, while those of the
Holy Grail developed into a cycle — there were apocryphal
versions of every conceivable event in religious or semireli-
gious history. Threads were tangled then which the wisest
of moderns have not been able to unweave; and incidentally,
this vigorous creativeness in sacred fields has furnished material for centuries of critical activity. But this is mere cavil-
ling. For it gave us, also, the only supremely great architecture of Christian Europe; it provided both atmosphere and
inspiration for six immortal schools of painting; and it bore
witness to an age vitally interested in the things of the spirit,
while as overwhelmingly virile and poetic as any the world
has known.

The surviving English lives of three popular virgin saints
— all clustering about the year 1230 — are excellently representative of this school of writing. Church history, in any
strict sense, they were not, and indeed were not understood
to be. The Lives of St. Katherine, Blessed Juliana, and St.
Margaret are scarcely comparable, for instance, to Bonaventura's familiar life of St. Francis of Assisi, nor to the still
more ancient history of Anselm by Eadmer of Canterbury.
Instead, they were the forerunners of those immense cycles
— ever hovering on the borderland between romance and
religion, beauty (or sometimes fantasy) and truth — known
later as the Legendaries. Their characteristics, of course,
varied. There is a noble dignity in the tale of how "went the

blessed maiden Katherine, crowned to Christ, from earthly pain, in the month of November, the 25th day . . . in the day and at the time that her dearly beloved Jesus, our Lord, gave up His life upon the cross for her and for us all." Perhaps because Katherine of Alexandria was so eminently an intellectual saint, her fabulous biography has contrived to appeal quite as much to the head as to the heart. But in the life of little St. Margaret, the English scribe has given free rein to fancy, and one recognizes all the machinery of romance. The medieval — or, indeed, the modern — reader must search far for a more zestful anecdote than the following. Margaret, imprisoned for her faith, has somewhat ill-advisedly besought God that she may *see* any invisible demons who may be lurking near, and her foster-mother, peering through a peephole of the dungeon, beholds the result:

There came out of a corner hastily toward her an unwight of Hell in a dragon's form, so grisly that it terrified them that saw it. That unseely-one glistened as if it were overgilt; his locks and his long beard blazed all of gold, and his grisly teeth seemed of swart iron, and his two eyes more burning than stars or than gemstones, and broad as basins. In his y-horned head, on either side of his high hooked nose, thrust smothering smoke of most dreadful kind, and from his sputtering mouth sparkled fire out; and so long reached his tongue that he swung it all about his neck, and it seemed as though a sharp sword went out of his mouth, that glistened like gleaming death and live lightning. . . . He stretched him and started toward this meek maiden, and yawned with his wide jaws ungainly upon her, and began to croak and to crink out his neck, as he would foreswallow her altogether. If she was afeared of that grisly grim one it was not much wonder.

Margaret's hue blenches with terror, and she forgets that all this is but an answer to her prayer. So she smote smartly down her knees to the earth and lifted her hands on high toward Heaven, and with this prayer to Christ called:

Invisible God, full of all good, whose wrath is so dreadful that Hell's fiends and the heavens and all quick things quake before it; against this aweful wight, that it harm me not, help me, my Lord. Thou wroughtest and wieldest all worldly things, they extol and praise Thee in Heaven, and all that dwell upon the earth, the fishes that in the floods float . . . *etc., etc.**

It is — like all of St. Margaret's! — a very long and comprehensive prayer; but it touches more than once upon sublimity and high poetry. And it proves that the religious element of the story, if not quite the primary interest, was at least earnest and authentic.

But this brings us to another side of the subject — the more personal, lyrical side. In spite of all its external violence and confusion, there was never an age when mystical love had more completely enthralled first the French, then the English heart, nor when it found more passionate expression. There was never an age when poet and priest (those two seers of the race) were more universally *one*. Innumerable songsters, modern as well as medieval, have found inspiration in the joys and sorrows of Mary the Virgin Mother; so that one may almost say, merely *to be* a poet is to be sensible of that tender and mystical and essentially *poetic* attraction which radiates from the Blessed Among Women. *Our tainted nature's solitary boast, Mystical Rose, Mary of the seven-times wounded Heart, Star of the Sea, Mother of the Fair Delight* — so have Christian poets, both within and without the fold, saluted her. But in certain anonymous English Marian poems of the twelfth and thirteenth centuries, we recognize a quite distinctive fragrance: something of its

Life of St. Marherete. Early English Text Society Publications, Vol. XIII.

cultured and exotic sweetness had no doubt been distilled in the gardens of Provence, but none the less it is spontaneously racy and national. This "maiden mother mild" (it was always the mildness which appealed in those strife-full days!), this bright Queen of men and angels, was never far from the vision of monk or Christian knight. The medieval mind, moreover, was not in the least afraid of that very ugly word "Mariolatry," and it confused the terms of divine and human love with most artless and engaging simplicity. So she was lauded in uncounted prayer-poems, but probably in none more characteristic than the

GOOD OREISUN OF OUR LADYE

Christ's mild Mother, Seynte Marie,
My life's true light, my lov'd Ladye,
To thee I bow, my knees I bend;
And my heart's blood to thee I send.

Soul's light thou art, and heart's true bliss,
My life, my hope, my shield I wis.
Thee will I laud with all my might
And sing thy lovesong by day and night,
For my soul thou hast holpen in many wise,
And led from Hell into Paradise. . . .

Thus vigorously opens up the poem, and figures of praise and love crowd fast upon one another. There is no woman like to this woman — high is her royal seat upon the Cherubim, before her beloved Son, within the Seraphim. Merrily the angels sing and carol before her, although no whit understanding the height of her bliss. Her children are as red as the rose and as white as the lily, her friends are as rich kings

crowned with gemstones; and with them evermore is day
without night, song without sorrow, peace without strife: —

> Behold, the Heaven is full of thy bliss,
> And the middle-earth of thy gentleness.
> Not one who calls thy help may miss,
> Such is thy grace and mildheartedness.

The poet proceeds, very humbly, to declare his sins and his
unworthiness of this Ladye's favor; none the less her love
has brought him into slavery, and he forsakes now all those
evil things which formerly were dear to him:

> Before thy feet will I lie and plead
> Till pardon I have of my misdeed.
> Thine is my life, my love is thine,
> All the blood of my heart is thine,
> And if I dare say't, *thou*, Ladye, art *mine*!

It is not a brief work (one hundred and sixty-eight verses),
but the ardor and vigor of appeal never for one moment
falter. Mary's intercession is besought, to obtain God's forgiveness at the hour of death; she is called upon to wash and
clothe the soul through her wide-spreading mercy. And the
poem ends with a most ingenuous prayer that God Almighty
may bring His, monk into gladness and to the vision of this
Ladye in her beatitude; and that all his friends may be the
better for this English lay which he has sung to them!

The *Oreisun* is very full of color and charm, of imagination and warm human feeling. Representative both in its
beauties and in its excesses, it mirrors faithfully that chivalrous and romantic devotion to the Mother of God which per-
meated life through the later Middle Ages. Ruskin saw in it a
very font of virtues — the exaltation of womanhood, of gentleness and purity, the glorification of the family ideal for

prince and for peasant. Cardinal Newman has pointed out how, among all nations, it has served as the most potent protection for the supreme dogma of the Divinity of Mary's Son. But at the time there was something flowerlike in the unconsciousness with which the devotion developed, spreading into inevitable luxuriance on all sides. It was not a cult; it was not, save in rare instances, a literary convention; it was the medieval version of Gabriel's *Ave,* framed from the "lore of faithful hearts."

"We are alike meditating on the Incarnation, whether our direct theme be incarnate God or His Mother," wrote Aubrey de Vere of the deep and tender insight. And the Incarnation is one of the few fundamental Christian mysteries which does not force the contemplation of what the same critic has called "matter too aweful for poetry." By bringing the infinite and unutterable down to the compass of a Mother and her Child, it has subjugated the devotion and imagination of the ages. So there is really no better way to gauge the emotional sincerity of these Marian poems than by studying the contemporary prayers to our Lord. They are absolutely free from self-consciousness, they bear no trace of what we have grown to call English reticence, the floodgates are down — the passionate ardor of the human heart is poured out like spikenard at the feet of Jesus Christ and Him crucified! The *Wooing of our Lord,* an exceedingly interesting and well-sustained piece of alliterative prose, is one of the most famous of these works. It is superlatively romantic:

Who may not love Thy lovely face? What heart is so hard that may not melt at the remembrance of Thee? Ah, who may not love the lovely Jesu? For in Thee are all things gathered together that might ever make one man love-worthy to another! . . .

For His beauty and His riches, His wisdom and might, His liberality and surpassing nobleness of birth, His graciousness and gentleness and kinship with the children of men — for all these the soul is urged to choose Jesus as true lover. Is not He that keen warrior who did rob hell-house and deliver its prisoners, and brought them out of the house of death into His own jeweled bower, the abode of everlasting bliss? The emotional warmth, the intimate sensibility and tenderness which throughout pervade the *Wooing,* have led some critics to believe it the work of a woman — most probably a nun consumed by love of the Heavenly Bridegroom. It would be vastly interesting to accept this theory, but internal evidence militates against it. For the work was designed primarily not as a sentimental effusion but as a meditation upon the Passion; possibly for the use of some consecrated Spouse of Christ. And the conclusion very forcibly suggests the authorship of a spiritual director:

Pray for me, my dear Sister. This have I written because that such words often please the heart to think upon our Lord. And therefore when thou art in ease, speak to Jesu and say these words: and think as though He hung beside thee bloody on the rood; and may He, through His grace, open thy heart to the love of Him, and to ruth of his pain.*

Friar Thomas of Hales' *Love Rune* is by all odds one of the most artistic and exquisite of these devotional poems. It possesses real imaginative and lyric value, but the length forbids insertion in the present study, and no extract would be found satisfying. So as a final and thoroughly characteristic product of this union of romance and religion, let us consider the ecstatic

*Early English Text Society Publications. Vols. XXIX to XXXIV.

OREISUN OF OUR LOUERDE

Jesus, true God, God's Son! Jesus, true God, true man and true Virgin's child! Jesus, my holy love, my sure sweetness! Jesus my heart, my joy, my soul's healing! Jesus, sweet Jesus, my darling, my life, my light, my balm, my honey drop! Thou art all I trust in, Jesus my weal, my winsomeness, blithe bliss of my breast! Jesus, teach me, Thou art so soft and so sweet, and yet too so likesome and so lovely and so lovesome, that the angels ever behold Thee and yet are never satisfied to look upon Thee. Jesus all fair, before whom the sun is but a shadow, even she that loseth her light and becometh ashamed of her darkness before Thy bright face! Thou that givest her light and hast all that light, illumine my dark heart. Ah! Lord Jesus, Thy succor! Why have I any delight in other things than in Thee? Why love I anything but Thee alone? O that I might behold how Thou stretchedst Thyself for me on the cross! O that I might cast myself between those same arms, so very wide outspread! He openeth them as doth the mother her arms to embrace her beloved child. Yea, of a truth! And Thou, dear Lord, goest spiritually towards us, Thy darlings, with the same outspreading as the mother to her children. Each is beloved; each is dear; each places himself in Thy arms; each will be embraced. Ah! Jesus! Thy humility and Thy great mercy! O that I were in Thy arms, in Thy arms so outstretched and outspread on the cross! And may any one ever hope to be embraced between Thy blissful arms in Heaven, unless He previously here hath cast himself between Thy piteous arms on the Cross? Nay, of a truth; nay, let no man expect it. Through this low embracing we may come to the exalted one. O Loving Lord! he must follow Thy steps through soreness and sorrow to the abode of bliss and eternal joy. Let no man think to ascend easily unto the stars!*

Thus the oreisun flows on — with the rhythmic rise and

*Early English Text Society Publications. Vols. XXIX to XXXIV.

fall, the half-inebriating and mystic sweetness of an ever-swinging censer. And it is not the rapturous colloquy of some exalted saint or mystagogue. It is the prayer, nowise unique, of a nameless Churchman — perhaps a busy bishop like the probable author of the *Ancren Riwle,* perhaps an obscure monk like Jocelin of Brakelond. The work does not seem to have been thought extraordinary by the scribe who handed it down to us; for the unfinished fragment of the *Oreisun* is tucked into the Lambeth MS. among a collection of homilies — in a strange handwriting, and according to its editors, mainly to fill up the remaining folios.

Oh, yes; there is a vein of sentimentality through all these works. They are a little weak in the quality of artistic selection, they sometimes offend our own fine sense of fitness, they are saturated with a curious sensibility which already tends to the fantastic, and threatens later on to become morbid or metaphysical. But they teach us the meaning of Coventry Patmore's strange arraignment, that not one really good prayer has been written by Catholic or Protestant since the days of the "Reformation." And they give us the measure of a perfectly vital, unconscious, and untrammeled faith.

For how unerring the poetic insight, through all this quaintness and *naïveté* — how ardent and intimate the union with God! No doubt we moderns have gained as well as lost by "growing up," by becoming critical rather than creative, and correct rather than spontaneous; still we have lost something. What are we to think of the mystical culture of England at a time when popular devotion was so clothed and crowned? And that was the England of pageant and miracle play; the England which had known Thomas à Becket and was soon to know Chaucer; the England where romance met and kissed religion — before the revolt of Wycliff, before the scourge of the Rose Wars, or the sophistication of the Italian Renaissance.

Mr. George Meredith, that very modern and professedly "scientific" student of human nature, once remarked that: "If we let romance go, we exchange a sky for a ceiling." We shall never be able to let it go altogether, because it is as elemental as it is seemingly unreal; but we can, and do, push recognition of it from one field to another. We can build our wall so close and our ceilings so low that one student's lamp shall pierce every inch of the darkness. Meanwhile the sky is above the ceiling, and our vision alone is the loser. For if we would save that persistent human hunger for romance from debasement and triviality, we must not divorce it utterly from spiritual ideals. And if we wish our appreciation of religion to be vital, refreshing, inspirational, it is as well to remember what Mr. Chesterton insists upon calling "the thrilling romance of orthodoxy."

THE LEGEND OF THE HOLY GRAIL

ITALY had, indeed, her St. Francis, her Dante, her group of Florentines who were to inaugurate the glory of Christian painting — but so far as Northern Europe is concerned, the spiritual aspiration of the Middle Ages seems to have reached its two highest peaks in Gothic architecture and the legend of the Holy Grail. And the two share more in common than may appear superficially. Both flowered with what appeared a sudden luxuriance but was in reality the fruit of long germination. Both may be called direct by-products of Faith, art-expressions essentially rooted in the Catholic religion, while at the same time vast enough to include very human details of secular life and thought; the contemporary portraits, even the grotesques of Gothic carving — the endless chivalric combats and often far-from-edifying love episodes of the spiritual romance, for instance. And both, reaching their high-water mark between the thirteenth and fifteenth centuries, have remained sources of esthetic stimulus and limitless adaptation ever since.

The legend — or cycle — of the Holy Grail may be defined briefly as the story of the cup or chalice used by Christ at the Last Supper and First Eucharist, mysteriously identified with the vessel held by Joseph of Arimathea to receive the Sacred Blood as it fell from the body of his crucified Lord; still more mysteriously carried later on to the continent of Europe, even perhaps to England, where it wrought many miracles and became the object of an immortal quest before being taken up into Heaven sometime between the fifth and eighth centuries. The variations upon this theme are, of course, innumerable — one of the most persistent being the legend propagated by the Glastonbury monks for pious or political purposes, to the effect that the Grail, or Graal as it is in Old French (from the Latin *gradale*, a dish or cup), was not celestially assumed at all, but remained ever since hidden within the precincts of their own abbey. And naturally there have been, and probably always will be, similar claims of possessing or discovering the priceless relic — in Spain, in Antioch, and various other quarters of the earth.

The origins of the story are almost as cryptically shrouded and as controversially discussed as its later developments, or for that matter its esoteric significance. Three main theories claim groups of special scholars in their defense. The first and most obviously plausible is the hypothesis of its Christian inspiration, claiming that the romance grew, as the early mystery plays grew also, directly from the liturgy of the Church — that it was, in fact, a dramatic interpretation and extension of the Mass, given dramatic timeliness by the immense and vital interest in the whole doctrine of Transubstantiation during the twelfth and thirteenth centuries. The second supposition is that the story was adapted from pagan Celtic legends of a magic, all-sustaining cup or dish; and it claims some credibility — although not so much as the militant Dr. Nutt insists* — by the food-producing quality at-

Legend of the Holy Grail, by Alfred Nutt. Folk Lore Society.

[34]

tributed to the Grail in many versions and by the fact that Perceval, the Grail Knight, is referred to as "le Gallois" or the Welshman from the first. There is also a third, rather fantastic theory which has endeavored to link up the legend with ancient cults of the Vegetation Spirit, as in the Mysteries of Adonis or Eleusis or even Osiris, going so far as to find phallic symbols in both chalice and lance; but most scholars dismiss this as far-fetched and negligible. Without attempting to trespass upon the precincts of the Wise Men, we are probably safe in believing that the beautiful legend — with that of Psyche one of the most beautiful in all the world! — was founded upon Christian devotion to the Eucharist, slightly modified by more magical and material Celtic traditions, and given its characteristic form by the universal love for a quest or hunt. But there is always the possibility that it *may* have grown from some grain of fact; infinitely overgrown, of course, by the fictions of imagination, devotion and geography.*

Fortunately the literary sources of the story are more definitely traceable than its inspiration. They are two, both in Old French verse: the *Perceval* or *Conte del Graal* of Chrétien de Troyes, probably written between 1174 and 1190, and the *Joseph* of Robert de Borron, attributed to the end of the twelfth or beginning of the thirteenth century — the first citing, as Professor Bruce points out, the legend of the Grail's existence, the second attempting to amplify and explain it. The story of the elect Grail Knight is only a part of Chrétien's work and may have been his own invention or a redaction from some earlier source now lost; in any

---

*In any study of the origin and development of the Grail legends Dr. James Douglas Bruce's monumental work, *The Evolution of Arthurian Romance* (The Johns Hopkins Press), is absolutely invaluable.

case it starts out with gracious *naïveté* to tell how in the springtime Perceval, the widow's son, hunting in the forest, is suddenly confronted by a company of knights. These he at first fancies to be devils, against whom his mother has warned him; but later decides must, from their glittering accouterments, be God and His angels — until they duly explain that they are knights from King Arthur's court. When the fascinated boy describes this encounter to his mother she swoons from fear, recalling how his father and brother have been slain in combat. But seeing that Perceval is determined to seek adventure at Camelot, she gives him much good counsel concerning prayer and the service of ladies, while he sets out in his simple garb of a Welsh peasant with a dart as his only weapon.

At the court he is taken for a rustic fool, but Arthur is as kind as Kay the seneschal is cruel. The youth's first adventure is the seeking and slaying of an objectionable Red Knight whose armor he assumes; then for a while he sojourns with Gournemant, an old knight who instructs him in the practices of chivalry and gives him the worldly advice of not quoting his mother and not asking so many questions! Perceval's next visit is to the castle of Gournemant's lovely niece, Blanchefleur; who comes to his bedside weeping and telling how she is besieged by a knight so evil that she will slay herself rather than yield to him. Perceval, naturally enough, is deeply moved. He becomes the lady's lover and defender, and after vanquishing his rival sends him back to Arthur's court.

There is apparently an interval during which the young knight forgets all except his dream of earthly love. Then he breaks away from Blanchefleur to seek his mother — not knowing that she has already died from sorrow. Next comes the mysteriously exciting incident of his meeting with two men *fishing,* one of whom invites Perceval to accept hospitality in his castle near by. He rides on but can find no trace of the building, until all at once, as through a lifted cloud, it is revealed close beside him. Entering, he is disarmed, clad in a red robe, and led into the great hall where some four hundred men are sitting; while on a couch lies a venerable lord or king, evidently ill and wounded. A sword is presented to Perceval — and then follows the first recorded procession of the Holy Grail. First a squire crosses the hall bearing a bleeding lance, followed by two others bearing ten-branch candlesticks; next, a damsel carrying a Graal which shines so radiantly that it dims the candles as the sun dims the stars; and after her another maiden bears a silver plate or paten. Perceval is overcome with wonder, but afraid to inquire the meaning of these holy wonders, because of Gournemant's advice. Like many another, he decides to ask the fateful question tomorrow; and tomorrow is too late, for when he wakes he finds the castle deserted and has barely time to saddle and mount his horse before the drawbridge is snapped up behind him.

Coming then upon a damsel lamenting her dead knight beneath an oak tree, Perceval learns that the mysterious fisherman and his host of the night before are the same person, known as the Fisher King, sorely wounded through the thighs many years before and now finding his entire sustenance in the Holy Grail committed to his care. This maiden, hearing his name of Perceval or Percevaux le Gallois, declares that it might better be Perceval the Caitiff, since had his courage been sufficient to ask the meaning of the Grail mysteries, the king would have been healed and the whole country cured of an evil spell. From her he learns also of his mother's death; after which the puzzled and sorrowful youth passes on to other exploits.

In these he is so successful that presently the king and his whole court come out to seek him. And they find him deep in contemplation before a wounded goose in the snow — the drops of blood against that whiteness reminding him not of the mystic Grail procession but of his lost Blanchefleur! However, entreated gently by the gentle Gawain, he returns with the knights to Camelot. Here next day comes a hideous lady whose mission seems to be chiefly to berate poor Perceval again; so that he swears he will never sleep two nights in the same place until he has repaired his fault and discovered the secret significance of the Grail.

It is not until more than a thousand lines are consumed with Gawain's exploits that Chrétien returns again to the story of Perceval. Five years have passed and we find him utterly discouraged and consumed by futile adventures, having succeeded not at all in his holy quest. Presently he meets a group of knights and ladies dressed as penitents, who remind him that the day is Good Friday, when it is unseemly to ride in armor. He is persuaded to seek a holy hermit near by, who proves by a charmingly intimate touch to be his own uncle; and to him Perceval confesses that he has *forgotten God through grief* over his failure to learn mysteries of the Grail. There seems a deeply spiritual truth here; as also in the hermit's suggestion that his own sin — forgetfulness, the adventure with Blanchefleur, or the more comprehensive one of self-seeking? — which had caused his mother's death, was responsible also for his silence at the appointed moment, since through it he *lacked the grace* to speak. But the stricken knight is given absolution and much good advice by his hermit uncle, and in the fresh paschal season he starts out anew to continue the quest of the Sangraal. "The rest is silence," so far as Perceval is concerned, since the remainder of Chrétien's poem is concerned with Gawain.

Messire Robert de Borron's metrical romance of *Joseph* might be described as a prelude to *Perceval,* written after the play — just as some popular hero's youth and antecedents are still related for public consumption hot upon the heels of that hero's first exploit. And with truly medieval thoroughness, de Borron begins his poem with the life and death of Christ Himself, His betrayal by the "seneschal" Judas, and the bestowal of His body, together with the holy and historic chalice, by Pilate upon Joseph of Arimathea. Reverently are we told how the Sacred Blood flowed again as Joseph and Nicodemus washed His wounds; then of Jesus' descent into Limbo and His resurrection. Joseph, imprisoned by the Jews, is visited by Christ, who brings for his comfort the luminous Grail, announcing that it shall be guarded by three persons — evidently himself, his brother-in-law Bron, and Bron's son Alain. Our Lord then gives a long dissertation upon the Blessed Sacrament, declaring the bread and wine to be verily His Flesh and Blood and explaining the orthodox symbolism of the Mass. And after promising that all who love this mystic chalice shall obtain their heart's desire in this life and everlasting joy in the next, He initiates Joseph into the *secrets of the Grail,* which we are later told are "sweet and precious, gracious and merciful."

Then follows the fanciful history of Vespasian, the Emperor's son, who, stricken with leprosy in Rome, is told by a pilgrim of Christ's miracles and healed by Veronica's kerchief. He and his imperial father set out for Jerusalem to avenge Christ's death; and after talking with Pilate, Vespasian is led to the Arimathean, who has subsisted many years

in his dungeon without food or drink. Joseph converts him
to Christianity — and being freed, starts into the desert with
his treasure the Grail and a company of friends and kins-
men. Most of these fall into sin, just as did the Children of
Israel; and Joseph is warned in prayer to set the chalice
openly before them, as Moses set the golden serpent. So a
table is arranged as at the Last Supper — upon it the Grail
and a *fish* caught by Bron — and the sinless, who alone are
permitted fellowship at this table, are rapt into an ecstasy
the others do not even suspect. One Moyses, the hypocrite,
forcing himself into their midst, is swallowed up by the
earth, while a Voice declares that the empty seat shall not
be filled until the third man of Joseph's line shall assume it;
evidently the genesis of the Siege Perilous. Later on the
aging Joseph, warned by an angel, transfers the guard-
ianship of the Grail to Bron, who is to be known as the Rich
Fisherman, instructing him long and carefully in the *Grail
secrets*. So after three days Bron turns *westward* with his
pilgrim clan; and it is revealed to him that while eleven of
his sons shall serve God in marriage, Alain, the twelfth, must
remain virgin and continue the sacred ministry of the Holy
Grail. After which de Borron, promising to return to their
history if he can find it in another book — that favorite subterfuge of medieval bards who, unlike their modern fol-
lowers, ever shunned the appearance of original creation! —
switches off to the ever-popular story of Merlin.

These two earliest fragments of the immortal romance
raise a thousand challenging questions. The relationship of
the two — consisting simply in the existence of the Grail,
the character of a mysterious Fisherman, and the general
command to travel west — does not at first seem very close.
But what was chiefly necessary was to identify the Grail, to

explain its presence in Europe, and to form a *liaison* between its adventures and the already regnant Arthurian cycle; after this, the details of the quest might be left to themselves for development. Whether Chrétien and de Borron drew from lost French or Latin originals is not particularly important, since both undoubtedly drew upon the riches of tradition. The really significant fact is that the Grail romance came precisely when, precisely because, men wanted it. For it was during that profoundly germinal twelfth century that the whole conception of the Blessed Sacrament became, as Cardinal Newman later expressed it, *magnified* in the Church. After the doctrine of Transubstantiation — immemorially treasured, of course, by the Faithful — had been formally defined by the Fourth Lateran Council in the year 1215, it immediately inspired the classic devotion of a Thomas Aquinas and a Bonaventura. But as the love of poets and people had preceded this official definition, so it flourished with new luxuriance after it; and it was part of the medieval psychology that where it loved it wove a romance — and after that another romance.

One of the most interesting, and one of the earliest after those two parent-sources in French, was the *Parzival* of the Bavarian knight Wolfram von Eschenbach. It is supposed to have been written during the first fifteen years of the thirteenth century and is of an admirable completeness, including the *Perceval* almost *in toto,* while adding a highly embroidered history of the Grail knight's parentage and a happy conclusion to his quest. But it has two characteristic differences, one apparently founded upon a faulty translation of the old French, the other upon a more domestic Teutonic viewpoint. For Wolfram, evidently misunderstanding Chrétien's graal, interprets it as a stone — possibly having in mind the altar stone — upon which every Good Friday his mystic dove descends with the Holy Wafer, and which then has power to supply its votaries with food as well as youth and immortality. This precious relic we find intrusted to a group of knights conspicuously resembling, as Dr. Bruce points out, the Knights Templars, at the castle of Munsalvaesche (seemingly the Spanish Montserrat or Monsalvat, with which, as with Glastonbury, legend has associated the Grail), ruled over by the Grail King. It is eloquent of Wolfram's nonascetical ideal that this spiritual and temporal leader — a kind of abstract, supra-territorial Pontiff — is, like many of his knights, permitted to marry; and that Parzival's own wife and his two sons. Lohengrin and Kardeiz, share his final vision of the Holy Grail.

An enormous expansion and diffusion of the story came during this thirteenth century. One of the most curiously imaginative variants — and one which the Celtic zeal of Dr. Nutt and others believes even earlier than Chrétien's work — is the Welsh *Peredur,* found in the famous collection of the *Mabinogion.* In it the pagan strain predominates, for while it largely follows the *Perceval,* a cryptic dish bearing a bleeding head is substituted for the Grail, and the motive of human vengeance for that of the Christian quest. Another rather unique version is the French metrical romance known as *Sone de Nausay,* in which the Grail castle has become a full-fledged monastery in charge of thirteen monks, its founder, the Fisher King, is identified as Joseph of Arimathea himself, and the locale of the whole is Norway. And as with other great romances of that intimately interrelated age, there were redactions of the story in Italian, Spanish, Dutch, *et cetera.*

By this time the nobility could generally depend upon

reading as well as upon the songs of the minstrels for their
diversion, so we find prose romances becoming everywhere
popular. The so-called Vulgate Cycle gives us the *Estoire del
Saint Graal* — known also as the *Grand Saint Graal* — a
lineal descendant of *Joseph,* and the *Queste del Saint Graal,*
a descendant of Chrétien's epic and the chief source of
Malory's. In the first of these, Josephes, the virgin son of the
Arimathean, supplants his father as keeper of the Grail; in
the second the immaculate Galahad is substituted for Perceval. These changes are, of course, highly significant. Ever
since the time of Hildebrand the Holy See had been fighting
hard to impose the ideal of celibacy upon the clergy of the
western Church; and undoubtedly the romance of the Grail,
whose hero was *par excellence* a knight sworn to the service
of the Eucharist, was siezed upon as both symbol and stimulus of this ideal — Galahad becoming more and more the
apotheosis of the perfect priest, guardian of the sacred chalice, initiated into its secrets and officer of its perpetual
sacrifice.

This sacerdotal aspect is stressed even at the expense of
the knightly in the chaste romance of *Perlesvaus* or *Perceval
le Gallois,* translated from an anonymous French prose MS.
of about 1220 by Sebastian Evans as the *High History of the
Holy Grail.* Here we are introduced to a Perceval (oddly
enough the old name is retained) described as the nephew
of the King Fisherman, making his home from the very
start in the Grail Castle and only occasionally leaving his
devotions for outside adventure. Presently he returns to this
"most holy castle" permanently, leading a religious life with
his mother and sister and surrounded by a company of godly
hermits. It is all so very pious, and so very domestic, that it

rather misses the mysterious thrill of the usual Quest legends: until, the others having died, Perceval is warned that the Grail shall appear there no more, and departs to seek it in a ship bearing one white sail signed with a red cross. What happened to him or to the blessed relic we are not told — only, by a touch of exquisitely delicate imagination, that all who ever after came near the abandoned castle were filled with strange joy.

By the fifteenth century the essential features of the Grail legends were fixed as definitely as they were ever to be, and the years from 1450 brought two important versions in English. The first was a *History of the Holy Grail* adapted by one Henry Lonelich or Lovelich, a "skynner," from the Sire de Borron, and following that early *Joseph* and the later *Estoire* with amplifications. When not overdiffuse it has a certain dramatic quality, as in its tale of the Grail-bearers crossing the sea to Britain —

> So upon the water went they there
> As though upon the dry ground they were —

and it describes quite definitely Josephes' eventual burial, presumably with the Grail itself, at Glastonbury.

But it remained for Malory's *Morte d'Arthur,* that storehouse of Arthurian romance, to crystallize the Quest into one of the masterpieces of English literature; and after Sir Thomas nobody would be likely to write or think of the immortal relic without an intensely spiritual motivation on one hand, and on the other an intimate identification with the Round Table knights. Yet it is not until Book XI — after the tragic story of Tristram and la Beale Isoud — that the first reference to the Grail theme is made by a hermit visiting Camelot, who announces that he who shall claim Merlin's empty seat, the Siege Perilous, will soon be born upon earth.

Then follows the history of Launcelot's adventures in the country of Corbin with King Pelles, a "cousin nigh of Joseph of Arimathie." Here, as they sat at table, "there came in a dove at a window and in her mouth there seemed a little censer of gold. And therewithal there was such a savour as all the spicery in the world had been there. And forthwithal there was upon the table all manner of meats and drinks that they could think upon. So came in a damsel passing fair and young, and she bare a vessel of gold betwixt her hands; and thereunto the king kneeled devoutly and so did all that were there." Launcelot, held back by none of the shyness that had so fatally deterred the earlier Perceval, demands the meaning of the ceremony, and is told by the king that his treasure is "the richest thing that any man hath living. And when this thing goeth about, the Round Table shall be broken; and wit thou well . . . this is the holy Sangreal that ye have here seen."

Ironically enough, the next episode is that in which through the witchery of Dame Brisen, who knows of his "faith unfaithful" to the Queen, Launcelot is lured into mating with Pelles' beautiful daughter Elaine — from which clandestine union was to be born the long-prophesied Galahad, "that should prove the best knight of the world." About a year later the faithful Bors (called in earlier versions Bohort), visiting Corbin, recognizes the babe as Launcelot's son, and as he kneels beside Elaine is himself granted the Grail vision. In fact it is the mysterious Grail maiden who declares: "This child is Galahad, that shall sit in the Siege Perilous, and achieve the Sangreal, and he shall be much

better than his father was, Sir Launcelot du Lake." Before
Sir Bors departs from the castle he witnesses once again that
strange sacramental procession — which this time includes
four children with tapers and an old man bearing a censer
in one hand and a spear in the other; who bids him warn
his cousin Launcelot that though he surpasses all worldly
knights, yet because of his sin he shall fail in the final quest
of all. Even Bors is permitted only to peer through the doorway of a brightly lighted room, where one vested as a bishop
kneels before an altar of silver, when the glory of a sword
suspended above his head — so reminiscent of Eden's gates!
— strikes him temporarily blind.

Many of the most parabolic and arresting details of the
Grail are here perpetuated by Malory. In the first place the
identity of the sacred vessel is revealed beyond all dispute;
while the aged man once again suggests Joseph of Arimathea, and the kinship between this procession and the liturgy
of the Mass is implied by candles, incense, and altar — even
the symbolic spear being used of course, in some of the
oriental liturgies. The seeming incongruity of the *maiden*
bearing the Grail, persistent from the time of Chrétien de
Troyes — although in certain rare variants we find the holy
vessel borne upon the horns of a white stag* — has never
been satisfactorily explained: probably she was a survival
from some primitive tradition of Celtic paganism, like the
food-producing quality of the relic; and she may have been
retained by Christian poets either from a chivalrous desire
to include woman as well as man in the Grail fellowship,
or as a mystical symbol of the Blessed Virgin bearing Christ.
Certainly there is nothing particularly consecrated in the

*Cf. *The Arthurian Legend in Italian Literature,* by Edmund G. Gardner
(E. P. Dutton and Co.).

old king and his daughter, who are the official custodians of the relic; but in all these versions there is a passionate anticipation of the pure knight who shall eventually be worthy to claim its ministry. And both Lonelich and Malory undoubtedly suggest a profoundly human paradox in their insistence that the child "begotten in sin" shall become the knight surpassing all others in sanctity — Galahad, who adds supernatural virtues to the natural courage and loyalty of his father, Launcelot. It may even be an unconscious or subconscious prophecy of Patmore's doctrine, implied by Dante and underlying all chivalric devotion, that human love is the *precursor* which finds its true flower and fulfillment in love divine.

But there is no denying that in its general attitude toward sex the *Morte d'Arthur* betrays a good deal of confusion between pagan and Christian morality. This confusion — which after all has not been confined to the Middle Ages! — is poignantly evident in the story of the abandoned Elaine who, loving Sir Launcelot "out of measure," dons her most gorgeous clothes and dares to hunt him up at Camelot. She and Guinevere show each other "good cheer by countenance, but nothing with hearts" at first; and after Elaine's enchantments have achieved another rendezvous with the knight, the Queen's jealous rage drives them both from the court. Then the knight Percevale (whom Malory also includes in the romance) and Launcelot's brother start out to seek their peerless leader; and when both are wounded in combat it is the Grail vision — scarcely seen this time, but apprehended by that mysterious spicy fragrance — which heals them in answer to prayer. And Sir Launcelot himself, found distraught by Elaine, is restored to his right mind by being placed to sleep in a room next to the sacred chalice.

After an interval of several peaceful years, the knight is discovered and persuaded to return to Court. Elaine, knowing this parting to be their last, grieves sorely, but tells Launcelot that at the coming feast of Pentecost she will send her son and his — the Galahad now fifteen winters old — to be dubbed knight by his hand. And when the eve of the feast comes, Launcelot is indeed called away to a convent in the forest; where among the kneeling nuns (for all the world as in Abbey's Boston painting!) he sees the young Galahad, "passing fair and well made and seemly and demure as a dove, with all manner of good features." And he confers upon him the high order of knighthood, praying God to make the boy as good as he is beautiful.

There is finely sustained suspense in Malory's story of that Pentecost celebration. Arthur and Guinevere, returning from the minster, find each knight's name in golden letters above his place at the Round Table, and on the Siege Perilous a script declaring that four hundred and fifty-four years after the Passion of Christ shall come he who must claim it. When all are seated, the doors and windows of the banquet hall close of themselves: and after a breathless pause Galahad, all in red, without sword or shield, is led in by an aged man, who announces that he brings a young knight of king's lineage and kin to Joseph of Arimathea, "whereby the marvels of this court and of strange realms shall be accomplished." As the youth sits augustly in the Siege Perilous, it is suddenly discovered to bear his own name. . . . So the king takes Galahad by the hand, and all the knights "wist not from whence he came, but all only by God; and said, This is he by whom the Sangreal shall be achieved." But it is not until after evensong, when all are again gathered together for supper, that the relic comes as it were to sum-

mon its predestined knight. There is the "cracking and crying of thunder," while the hall is pierced with a sunbeam
seven times brighter than the day: "and all they were
alighted of the grace of the Holy Ghost. Then began every
knight to behold other . . . fairer than ever they saw afore.
. . . Then there entered into the hall the Holy Grail covered
with white samite, but there was none might see it nor who
bare it" — with the usual accompaniments of sweet odors
and every manner of food. And first the impulsive Gawain,
then one hundred and fifty of the Round Table knights,
rise up and swear to lay aside all earthly aims and follow
this quest until they behold the Grail more openly. A year
and a day shall they ride, unless it is shown to be God's will
that they turn back; and there is great grief in the hearts of
the "ladies and gentlewomen" who may not bear them
company — especially with the Queen, who sees Launcelot
go from her side and knows well enough that Galahad is
his son; and with Arthur, who knows that never again on
earth shall so fair a company be gathered together. For as
usual, it is the best who undertake the hardships of the pilgrimage — the worst who remain behind to work their own
selfish ends. "And so," continues this incomparable chronicle, "they mounted upon their horses and rode through the
streets of Camelot; and there was weeping of the rich and
poor, and the king turned away and might not speak for
weeping."

Then, since none knew where the Grail might be found,
"every knight took the way that him liked best." Galahad,
staying overnight at a certain White Abbey, is given a shield
whereon "the gentle knight" Joseph of Arimathea long ago
imprinted a cross with his own blood, and so starts off upon
"many journeyings forward and backward." The old book

recounts his visit to the Castle of Maidens, where he rescues the imprisoned damsels from seven evil knights evidently representing the Seven Deadly Sins, and mixes in with the marvels charmingly contemporary pictures of medieval life. But it gives no visit of the young knight to the Grail castle, no poignant episode of the *unasked question*. For unlike the Perceval of the earlier versions, Galahad is now from the first a faultless knight, incorruptibly chaste, one who "sinned never" and slays no man lightly.

Constantly over against his somewhat dazzling virtue is set the figure of his struggling, heroic, never wholly penitent father, Launcelot. One unforgetable picture shows the wearied knight falling asleep by an empty chapel and granted that ancient mystic vision of the sick man borne upon a litter, who, crying out to God for help, is suddenly visited and healed by the Sangreal. But Launcelot, so quick in worldly quests, is overwhelmed by the spiritual apparition; and may not even rise in the divine Presence until he hears a Voice commanding him to depart from that holy place, since he is "harder than is the stone, and more bitter than is the wood, and more naked" than the fig tree cursed by our Lord. So at dawn — when the little "fowls" are beginning to sing — he seeks out a holy hermit whom he beseeches to "hear his life." In that agonized confession he reveals how he has loved Guinevere "immeasurably and out of measure long," for her sake rather than God's doing battle "were it right or wrong." The good man gives Launcelot not only the obvious counsel, but points out that He who has bestowed upon the knight "fairness and seemliness . . . wit, discretion to know good from evil . . . prowess and hardihood," will suffer his neglect no longer, but — like the

Hound of Heaven — is determined to possess his heart whether he will or no. And Launcelot, cleansed by contrition and the priest's shrift, goes out humbly on foot to continue his quest of the Grail; being driven to still greater penance later on by another hermit who prophesies to him, "Seek it ye may well, but though it were here ye should have no power to see it."

"Celerity," as Shakespeare once remarked, "is never more admired than by the negligent"— which perhaps explains this badgering of Launcelot's fault in a romance otherwise reeking with episodes of amorous adventure, both lawful and unlawful. It is all part of the stress, possibly even the overstress, upon virginity by which medieval idealists were striving to cleanse a youthful society whose sins are flaunted frankly enough by a Chaucer or a Boccaccio. While the orthodox Church seems to have suspected that the Grail legends reflected not infrequently the theology of the poets rather than the theologians, while motherlike she half resented the intrusion of romance so close to her pivotal doctrine of the Eucharist, we have seen how she yet found in the legend an incomparable opportunity to impress art in the service of quite angelic virtue: absolute virginity for the chosen knight, the high priest of the Blessed Sacrament, purity for all who would make up its confraternity. So Malory's Percevale, who is one of Galahad's chosen companions, is as celibate as Galahad himself; while the third of the trio, Sir Bors, mighty in faith, is chaste but for one love in the past — possibly an echo of the original *Perceval* of Chrétien de Troyes.

For increasingly we find the meaning of the Grail quest revealed, as Lizette Andrews Fisher points out in her illuminating study* — not only as a "mystic intuition" but a "direct knowledge" of the miracle of Transubstantiation: St. Angela da Foligno's understanding of *how God comes into the Sacrament,* a revelation so precious that it requires uncommon purity of body, mind, and will in the recipient. Thus Malory's good knights, Gawain and Sir Ector, are warned away from the quest by the very hermit who gives them absolution. "Ye go to seek what ye shall never find, for it is the secret thing of our Lord Jesus Christ," he tells them: "Truly there be a hundred such as ye." Many a thousand, many a million of everyday Christians, one fears — always and in every century the vast majority of the struggling, faulty Faithful! For it is but the chosen few through the long ages of our *enigmatic vision* who even suspect, with Lionel Johnson,

> How deep within the liturgies
> Lie hid the mysteries;

and fewer still who attain to them this side of Eternity.

Meanwhile Galahad is led by the grace of God and an unknown maiden — *Dieu et ma dame,* as the chivalric formula had it! — to a mysterious ship where Bors and Percevale await him. Here the lady is revealed as Percevale's own wise and fair sister, and all make great joy of one another. But presently, after a warning to be in "perfect faith," they are transferred to a still greater ship said to have been built by Solomon for his wife: *which* wife the legend does not specify, but it remarks that she was evil enough to destroy his belief in other women! The next few chapters are so steeped in magic and allegory that no one, except that sibylline sister

The Mystic Vision in the Grail Legend and in the Divine Comedy, by Lizette Andrews Fisher (New York: Columbia University Press).

of Percevale, could hope to disentagle the significance. But there is a telling touch in the description of David's sword — which only Galahad, of course, is able to draw from its sheath — where we are told that the scales of its haft come from the bones of two strange beasts: one insuring against all *weariness,* the other imparting to its bearer so much *will* that he thinks of no joy nor sorrow of the past but only upon the work before him. And it is perhaps not hard to understand why, just when this chaste romance with Percevale's unnamed sister — the only romance permitted Galahad in these later versions of the quest — reaches the point where she has woven a girdle from her own hair for his sword, and has foretold the eventual healing of his grandsire, King Pelles, while he swears himself "her knight all days," their parting should be ordained. It is as a saint and martyr that she goes, after they reach the coast of Scotland; yielding herself for the healing of a stranger lady who may be cured only by a dish full of blood from a "clean virgin in will and in work." And sorrowfully the three knights place the body of their Egeria in a sailless ship draped in black — which she promises shall be waiting to welcome them in the harbor of the mystical city of Sarras.

A little later Launcelot, being commanded to enter this ship, finds there "the most sweetness that ever he felt," and is sustained by the Holy Ghost without mortal food. Presently he is joined upon the barge of peace by Galahad, and they live together for half a year, telling each other their adventures "with many a friendly word, as kin would." But neither in domestic joy nor in the memory of love foregone may Galahad, the Divine Wanderer, dwell. For there appears to him a white knight leading a white charger, and saying: "Sir, ye have been long enough with your father, come out of the ship and start upon this horse and go where the adventures shall lead thee in the quest of the Sangreal." To penitent father and innocent son it is revealed that they shall meet no more upon earth, so they kiss tenderly and part with prayerful blessings.

For both, indeed, the long quest is almost at an end. Launcelot is borne by the ship back to Pelles' castle, where he finds all doors open and hears singing of unearthly beauty. From the king, old and ill, he learns that Elaine, the mother of Galahad, is dead; and here, where he has had his first cryptic vision of the Grail, he has also his last. Upon an altar of silver he sees the sacred vessel resting, covered with red samite, while a priest stands at the sacring of the Mass with angels kneeling round about. But as Launcelot would press nearer, he is smitten by a breath of fire and falls unconscious; after which he rises up with mingled joy and sorrow, knowing that he may achieve no fuller vision in this life. So he returns to Camelot — to the Queen who has mourned for him, and the King who mourns more than half of the Round Table Knights lost or slain in their hopeless adventure.

Meanwhile Galahad, after "many journeys in vain," is reunited with Percevale and Bors, and together they, too, travel to Corbin. So at last is reënacted the old miracle of the maimed king — Pelles healed by his grandson through the application of blood dripping from the holy spear. And here the supreme vision denied to Launcelot is granted to the faithful trio. Kneeling before that silver altar, they see Mass celebrated by none other than Joseph of Arimathea; and at the consecration "there came a figure in likeness of a child, and the visage was as red and as bright as any fire, and smote himself into the bread." Yet it is the vision not of a child but of a man, with all the signs of Christ's Passion upon him, who rises from out the Grail. . . . Transubstantiation can go no further in visibility — only it remains for the Christ brought down among men to speak to them. . . .This He does gently, saying to the three: "My knights and my servants and my true children, which be come out of deadly life into spiritual life, I will now no longer hide myself from you, but ye shall see now a part of my secrets and of my hidden things." From His own wounded hand they receive His sacramental Body — from His own lips the commission to bear the blessed Grail overseas to the golden city of Sarras, away from men no longer worthy to possess it.

So on the morrow they set sail, carrying with them both Grail and spear, before which they daily make their prayers. But for Galahad even a life grown wholly sacramental begins to pall; initiated into the mystery of the Eucharist — the mystery of the Church Militant — he would press on to the mysteries of the Church Triumphant, Christ's dual nature and the Holy Trinity. And after they reach Sarras, where the pure body of Percevale's sister awaits them, and where Galahad reigns for one year as king, his hunger for eternity is satisfied. Once again comes Arimathean Joseph, once again the knights receive communion from his hands. Then Galahad trembles as the final initiation begins, but his prayer is "Now, blessed Lord, would I not longer live if it might please Thee, Lord." Tenderly he goes to Percevale and Bors, kissing them and commending them to his father Launcelot. Then, as he kneels, his soul departs suddenly, and the faithful friends behold a multitude of angels bearing it up to heaven. "Also the two fellows saw come from heaven a hand, but they saw not the body. And then it came right to the Vessel, and took it and the spear, and so bare it up to heaven. Sithen was there never man so hardy to say that he had seen the Sangreal."

Percevale, the holy contemplative, departs to a monastery — but Bors, the holy man of action, returns to Camelot that all may know the quest has been achieved. There, among the gathering feuds of the knights, the renewed loves and quarrels of Launcelot and Guinevere, he lives on as stranger and pilgrim. For the high service of the Grail "may not lightly be forgotten," in Launcelot's own wistful words. One likes to believe that among its after-effects was the conversion of those hapless lovers — their sublime parting after Arthur's death, their "turning to perfection," and at long last their passing to the peace they had desired, but alas! too weakly sought.

Malory's story has been told at such length not merely because of its poignant power, but because it has become, for English readers at least, the definitive classic of the Grail. Professor Remy points out* the curious fact that "after the Renaissance, the Grail legend, together with most medieval legends, fell into oblivion, from which it was rescued when the Romantic Movement set in at the beginning of the nineteenth century." It was the latter half of that century which saw a sudden revival of the theme in no less than three separate arts. Incomparably the most interesting poetic version came from Tennyson, first in his early lyric of *Sir Galahad,* later in the mature spiritual beauty of *The Holy Grail.* This crowning glory of his *Idylls of the King* could never have been written had Victorian England not passed through the travail of the Oxford Movement, for it is amazingly steeped in Catholicism. In fact, it is a nineteenth-century version of Malory, highly etherealized, perhaps too vig-

Catholic Encyclopedia, "The Holy Grail," by Arthur F. J. Remy.

orously expurgated, substituting for the hard bright colors and vigorous humanity of medievalism a wealth of conscious imagery and a mysterious haze through which the past is less revived than evoked.

Tennyson's Arthur is almost as impeccable as Galahad himself; and instead of the erring Launcelot — to whom, however, as to Guinevere, he gives a haunting and pitiful reality — it is Percevale's sister, now a "holy nun," who has the first prescient vision of the Grail in England. Quite in the spirit of Malory is the king's warning that for most of his knights the quest will be a pursuit of "wandering fires," and Launcelot's last visit to the mysterious castle of Corbin, and Galahad's Transubstantiation vision. But Bors and Percevale are not permitted to come as close to the ultimate glory of the Grail as in the medieval version; with modern individualism, this is reserved for the virgin knight upon whose lips Tennyson had put the musical and dreamily pictorial meditation:

> Sometimes on lonely mountain-meres
>   I find a magic bark;
> I leap on board; no helmsman steers;
>   I float till all is dark.
> A gentle sound, an awful light!
>   Three angels bear the Holy Grail;
> With folded feet, in stoles of white,
>   On sleeping wings they sail.
> Ah, blessed vision! blood of God!
>   My spirit beats her mortal bars,
> As down dark tides the glory slides,
>   And star-like mingles with the stars.

It was characteristic of the wistful Verlaine that he should give us a wistful *Parsifal*, hearing the voice of little children as he walks, "king and priest," yet somewhat overburdened by the weight of spear and chalice; characteristic, too, that his *Saint Graal* should be a salutation to the Blood of Christ still flowing in love and pardon over France. There is an exotic note in both of these poems — as in the frail, fascinating Grail angel designed by Aubrey Beardsley for the Gollancz edition of the *Morte d'Arthur* during the 1890's. But it is Malory himself, when it is not his precursor Chrétien, who is responsible for the rich and thrilling perpetuation of the Grail Quest which Edwin Abbey has painted upon the walls of the Boston library.

The sublime musical setting given to the legend by Richard Wagner in 1882 harks back, in name at least, to Wolfram von Eschenbach, since its hero-knight — the "guileless fool" — is Parsifal, and the Grail castle is Monsalvat in the Pyrennees. But Wolfram's domesticity is superseded by an ideal of quite monastic and sacerdotal sanctity, whose betrayal brings a frightful heritage of pain and remorse; and the traditional emphasis upon virginity is carried so far that we find human love confused with evil magic in the persons of Klingsor the necromancer and Kundry the penitent enchantress. The eucharistic ceremony of Wagner's music drama has, to be sure, something of that esoteric and unorthodox quality which made the medieval Church more than once distrust these Holy Grail romances. Still its affinities with the Mass ritual are obvious — the miraculous suggestion of Transubstantiation is almost overpowering — while the piercing, soaring beauty of the music achieves precisely that sense of a battle against supernatural odds, crowned by supernatural ecstasy, which was the essence of the Grail quest.

That the reiterated *Secrets of the Grail* are the *Secreta* or

[58]

Canon of the Mass, and the uncovered vision of the Grail the comprehension or apprehension of the Real Presence, seems proved clearly enough, not only by the great company of scholars who hold to the Christian origin of the legend but still more finally by the enormous Christian significance of its whole later development. Professor Bruce believes the Fisher King, who has been so integral a part of the story from its dusky dawn, to be no other than Christ Himself, *bruised for man's transgressions*. But why may not this pathetic king — symbolically wounded "through the thighs," receiving his nourishment from the Blessed Sacrament, and awaiting cure from a holier hand — rather typify Humanity? And why may not the idea of that high but for the most part hopeless quest — that long and painful seeking for what may never on this earth be possessed — be at least partially a reflection of the tragic Crusades which alternately tore and transfigured medieval Christendom?

It is just because of these searching, troubling, multitudinous problems that the inner meaning of the story remains so challenging. For meaning we should, perhaps, substitute meanings — and then accept St. Augustine's profound and piquant preference for "as many meanings as possible." But after all, the essential, persistent significance of the Grail legend is the human quest of the divine. And it was an instinct so sound that it amounted to an inspiration when art bound it up inseparably with that Holy Eucharist which represents also the divine quest of the human.

TRISTRAM,
PERENNIAL HERO OF ROMANCE

THE Holy Grail *motif* was, of course, the most profound and sublime and mysterious legend of the
Arthurian cycle — but there seems no doubt that the story
of Tristram and Iseult was the best beloved. And inevitably,
since it gathered into itself and grew to symbolize the very
anguish and apotheosis of human passion: giving the medieval world in Tristram of Lyonesse the perennial hero of
romance, in Iseult of Ireland (to borrow Chaucer's playful
but pitiful paradox) the sinful, suffering "saint of Cupid."

It is interesting to remember that one of the first books
printed at Caxton's historic press in London — as early, in
fact, as 1485 — was Thomas Malory's immortal *Morte
d'Arthur,* fully one third of which was occupied with the
romance of Tristram and la Beale Isoud. The story was
already venerable, already what our modern literary com-
mercialism would describe as a "best seller." Indeed, with the
French versions of Chrétien de Troyes, Béroul, Thomas, and
Rusticien de Pise, and the German of Eilhard von Oberge
and Gottfried von Strassburg, it might have been so described from the thirteenth and late twelfth centuries; while
the tale is plausibly enough traced back to legendary British

— that is to say, Celtic — origin, colored by Viking details. No doubt the Wise Men are wise in identifying Mark with a certain King of Cornwall during the seventh, or possibly the ninth century, and Iseult "la Blonde" with a Norse princess of Ireland. But it scarcely matters. According to every poet worth listening to, the lovers worked out their destiny when Arthur reigned at Camelot: for the rest — like Percival or Galahad or Arthur himself — they are what the ages have wanted them to be. For if tradition, as Mr. Chesterton somewhere remarks "telescopes history," poetry both concentrates and interprets it.

While the great romance was, then, of northern origin and immensely popular in England, Germany, Spain, and Italy, the gentle tyranny of the French tongue was so inescapable during the Middle Ages that one must turn to France for its existing sources: many of which survive only in fragments, while Chrétien's celebrated version has not survived at all except in the pages of its imitators. But modern scholarship, and not less the modern reader of romance, owes an infinite debt to M. Joseph Bédier for his exquisitely harmonious redaction of the various and varying medieval versions — a redaction which so perfectly builds up a whole from the scattered parts that Gaston Paris could declare this *Roman de Tristan et Iseult** veritably "a French poem of the middle of the twelfth century, but composed at the end of the nineteenth." Seldom have art and scholarship been so happily and fruitfully wedded; and to give a *résumé* of Bédier's *"beau conte d'amour et de mort"* — which has recently been superbly Englished, but alas! also curtailed by Hilaire Belloc — is perhaps the best introduction to the whole romance in

*Renouvelé par Joseph Bédier (Paris: Piazza).

that fluid medieval form which is still the storehouse of our modern poets and dramatists.

"Once upon a time," when King Mark reigned in Cornwall, he was aided in war by his friend Rivalen of Lyonesse, who soon after took his sister Blanchfleur as wife. Nor was it a "marriage of convenience" (as there were too many, even then!) for the two loved "marvelously"; and when recalled to Lyonesse by another of those ubiquitous wars, Rivalen confided his bride in all tenderness to his steward Rohalt the Faith Keeper (*Le Foi Tenant*). But it was not long before he himself was slain — and the young stricken queen kept herself alive only long enough to bear and to kiss her little son, then fluttered out to join him in death. The child, so sadly born, was christened Tristan, and for safety brought up as one of Rohalt's own sons. But by Gouvernail he was instructed in all knightly arts: "the use of lance and sword and 'scutcheon and bow, and how to cast stone quoits and to leap wide dykes . . . and to hate every lie and felony and to keep his given word; and he taught him the various kinds of song and harp-playing, and the hunter's craft"* — so that when the youth, having been stolen by Norse pirates, was considerately dropped off on the coast of Cornwall, the cruder courtiers of his uncle were amazed at his accomplishments. And Mark himself adopted the boy with all devotion, although ignorant of his kinship until it was later revealed by the faithful Rohalt. In fact, so warm was the bond between uncle and nephew through these early versions of the story that Tristan voluntarily abandoned his own princedom, staying on in Cornwall with his squire Gouvernail.

Then occurred the fateful episode of the Irish knight Mor-

*Tristan and Iseult, by Joseph Bédier. Translated by Hilaire Belloc.

holt (or Morhaus), who came demanding tribute of King
Mark — and was defeated in bitter combat by young Tristan; returning to his country so sorely wounded that not all
the healing skill of his sister the queen and his royal niece
Iseult could save his life. Tristan, too, languished sadly with
a poisoned wound no Cornish leech could cure; until disguised as a harper, he set out for Ireland in one of those
sailless ships dear to medieval lore. It appears to have been
just the sort of wound Iseult la Blonde could heal (there were
others, later on, she could only share!) and presently he was
back in Cornwall, hale and only comfortably smitten; that
is to say, only sufficiently impressed by the princess' golden
hair to recommend her to his uncle, whom the barons were
urging to take a wife!

So once again Tristan departs for the Irish coast, this time
with a proper retinue of knights; and by way of favorable
introduction, he slays the worst of all Celtic dragons almost
as soon as he sets foot on shore. Once again wounded, he is
once again tended by the young Iseult — who this time recognizes him as slayer of her uncle Morholt, and is almost
fain to have his life in vengeance. Almost . . . but not quite:
for there is a kiss of peace between them — the first and the
last kiss of peace! And already the princess' heart must have
been touched, since she grieves in bitter humiliation when
she learns for whom Tristan comes wooing. Yet she consents
to Mark's suit (the medieval princess knowing her duty as
well as the modern!): and it is then that her mother — in a
moment of pity, perhaps, or of foreboding? — prepares that
magic potion which is essence, excuse and explanation of the
whole later story. The philter is confided to Brangein, the devoted handmaid of Iseult, to be drained by king and queen
on their wedding night: for, in the words of the old minstrel,

Those who drink of it must love with every sense and every thought, forever, in life and death.

There are dull days on shipboard — days of a dull resentment between Tristan and Iseult — then suddenly a torrid spell. And all unknowingly, the two, left alone, drink the cup of their destiny. It is worth noting that the first frank confession comes from the woman — after that, the inevitable. . . . And the penitent Brangein, discovering them in each other's arms, warns them that in the potion they have drunk *love and death*. Unquestioningly, the man and woman accept this bittersweet verdict, from which there is no further appeal, apparently, to free will or to grace. And it was accepted quite as unquestioningly, we may suppose, by not a few of their medieval readers, who shared the belief in magic philters which had come down from Pliny's day. Modern minds, correct and somewhat easily scandalized — unless they be so incorrect and uninhibited as not to be scandalized at all! — must learn tolerance by turning back to an older and higher parable, in which the good seed of the Husbandman and the evil seed of the Enemy were suffered to grow up until the final harvesting of an all-seeing God.

Iseult, arrived at Tintagel, lights up the old fortress-castle with her beauty "like the rising sun," and before long she is wedded to the blissfully ignorant Mark. Thanks to the vigilance and self-sacrifice of Brangein, the unhappy lovers are shielded and for awhile all goes well. But, as the old romance observes, love cannot be hidden; and it is discovered first by those who hate the lovers. They are spied upon by enemy knights — the king is warned — and Tristan banished from the court. But at all hazards he must bid the queen farewell; and here is introduced the famous, or infamous, episode of the flour sprinkled upon the floor of Iseult's chamber, with the footprints (in some versions it is the blood-stains from a wound in Tristan's leg) which betray his visit. This time Mark is so furiously convinced of the lovers' perfidy that he determines both shall be burned without trial. But "Hearken if the Lord God is full of pity," cries M. Bédier, with that blending of piety and sympathy so conspicuous in his medieval precursors: and at the last moment Tristan not only escapes himself but is able to rescue Iseult when the king, apparently unwilling to burn her, has delivered her over to the more shameful torment of the leper colony.

It is conspicuous that both continue to protest at least a technical innocence of Mark's charge — because they have been denied trial by combat, by ordeal, or by their peers (three forms recognized by medieval justice), and seemingly also because their drinking of the love potion had been an *involuntary* act. So, escaping to the forest, they wander together through two years of joy and hardship. Here follows the charming story of Tristan's little brachet, which tracks her master through fastnesses the knights could not pierce; the edifying story of the hermit Ogrin, who begs the half-distraught lovers to return to duty and the king; and the symbolic story of Tristan's sword, which Mark discovers lying between his wife and nephew as they sleep upon the ground, and which persuades him of their guiltlessness — the sword he then takes, leaving his own in its place as token of pity and proffered pardon. As usual, mercy prevails where justice cannot — or perhaps the rebels are worn out and beaten by life; at any rate they travel back to the good hermit and commission him to write their surrender to King Mark. "I do not say that I repent for having loved and for loving Tristan," cries the dauntless Iseult, kneeling at the holy man's feet, "but henceforth in body at least we shall be separated."

They are pardoned by the long-suffering husband — and Iseult really means it to be a final kiss which she gives Tristan with her ring of green jasper, just as he really means to start for foreign lands when he gives her his faithful little hound. But somehow, he tarries near by. — And it is well he tarries, since once again traitor knights poison the old king's mind, pointing out that his queen's honesty is not yet vindicated and suggesting that she and it be proved by the ordeal of red-hot irons! Iseult, who has never lacked courage and who seems to have acquired an almost presumptuous faith in God's mercy, accepts the challenge. Then, the old story tells how Tristan, duly warned, waits at the appointed spot disguised as a palmer, and is opportunely able to raise up his beloved as she stumbles upon the beach. And so, with the very finesse of all romantic sophistry, the queen swears upon the holy relics that she has never been in the arms of any man save those of Mark and this poor pilgrim — verifying her word to the shame of her accusers, by touching the hot irons unscathed.

No longer needed save by the heart of Iseult, Tristan at long last breaks away from Cornwall, seeking and finding adventures of every sort overseas. Some of the versions tell how he discovers a tiny enchanted dog bearing a marvelous bell whose music can banish all pain, and sends both back to his mistress; who, refusing any anodyne while he must suffer on, throws the magic bell into the sea. And all tell how, having fought for the king of Brittany, Tristan is persuaded to the apparent treachery of espousing the young princess, Iseult of the White Hands. But on his wedding night, the

jasper ring falls from his finger — bringing back such poignant memories of the *real* Iseult that before long he sails away
from his maiden bride and back to Cornwall.

Rumors of the marriage have, however, preceded him,
bringing what bitterness one may imagine to Mark's lonely
queen. So when he appears (disguised this time as a leper)
Iseult orders him driven away by the servants; for there is
nothing like the cruelty of a woman to the man she loves,
except the cruelty of a man to the woman he loves! Too
late, when he is gone, she is sorry, and dons sackcloth by
way of penance. But there is to be one more meeting — told
in the curious anecdote known as Tristan Crazed, or Tristan
the Fool — where the knight, assuming madness like Hamlet
and probably pushed half to madness, too, enters Tintagel
amid the jeers of the court, and is recognized first by the
adoring little hound, finally by his queen. Then there are
stolen, agonized embraces — their last on earth.

For Tristan, back again in Brittany, is wounded to death
in one of the ceaseless feuds. Knowing the end near, he dis-
patches his wife's brother, Kaherdin, with the jasper ring, to
summon his mate in love and in death; bidding him (with
an echo of the Theseus legend) carry white sails if Iseult be
with him, black if he comes alone. But Iseult of the White
Hands overhears their project and watches her moment for
revenge. Meanwhile Kaherdin has delivered his secret message at Tintagel, and Iseult, eluding the courtiers, is off with
him across the stormy seas. A tempest overtakes them — then
a calm through which they can make no progress. And as the
days mount up, the despairing queen has but one prayer —
"If God wills, if God wills" — even while a presentment
pierces her soul that He does not so will.

At last sea and sky are bright again, and the ship, bearing

its white banner of hope, is pushing into the Breton harbor. Then comes the piteous catastrophe — so like life and so unlike the necessities of romance that one feels it stamped by the seal of truth. For Tristan, too feeble himself to look through the window, demands the color of the approaching sail from his wife: and Iseult the "fair and simple" tells him *black*. So, turning his face to the wall, he cries out three times for his "friend," and dies uncomforted — paying, it may be, the price of all those past, forbidden comfortings!

Already the Cornish queen is mounting the castle stairs, while men draw back from her imperious beauty and imperious woe. "I shall better mourn than thou, for I have better loved than thou," she tells the shamed wife, taking her place by Tristan's side. And to the broken and contrite heart of Iseult, her God does not refuse the final prayer for death. Then the old, unhappy but never ungracious story tells how Mark buried the "star-crossed lovers" in his own chapel at Tintagel, at the right and left of the apse. But still they were too far apart: for during the night a flowering briar climbed from the tomb of Tristan to the tomb of Iseult, and would in no wise be separated ever again.

When, in the reign of Edward IV, Sir Thomas Malory enshrined this romance with the other Round Table legends in that miracle of Middle English prose, *Le Morte d'Arthur,* he borrowed copiously from French sources — no doubt those included by M. Bédier, and the supposed versions of Lucas de Gast and Robert or Hélie de Borron* as well, perhaps dipping also into shorter British fragments. But the form which

---

*Professor W. H. Schofield refers to these as the "Vulgate" and the "enlarged" *Tristan* respectively, in his *English Literature, From the Norman Conquest to Chaucer.*

his own personality so admirably colored is at once more complex and less complete than the story just recounted. His Tristram is the recognized idol of chivalry, a "harper passing all other," a superlative hunter and hawker and bugler, second to Launcelot alone as knight of the Round Table. "La beale Isoud" is the "fayrest mayde and lady of the world," a wise princess and a good queen save only in her allegiance to Tristram. In vivid contrast to the lovers stands the ignoble figure of Mark, a coward and traitor almost from the first. "King Fox" he is aptly called by Launcelot — and Malory assures us he was notorious as the "shamefullest king that liveth, a great enemy to all good knights." The queen's preference for her peerless Tristram is thus predestined — and all too easily pardonable, one needs to remember, with the magic might of the love potion taken into consideration, by both Malory and the "Christian reader" for whom he wrote. Moreover, by the artistic device of making uncle and nephew early rivals in the not-too-creditable wooing of a certain Cornish lady, after which "though there was fayre speech, love there was none" between them, his Tristram is spared the ignominy of betraying friend or benefactor. So, with quite ingenuous delight, the meetings and partings of these hapless and rather unscrupulous lovers are distributed between the innumerable tourneys of Tristram and his brother knights. Malory brings into his version the incident of the Magic Horn to prove the queen's infidelity, and is rather partial to Sir Palomides, the pagan knight who would like to be Tristram's rival in love and in arms; he shows Isoud herself bidding her lover seek the Breton princess for cure of his wound, and makes the subsequent madness of Tristram (which strongly resembles the madness of Launcelot

after a rebuke by Guinevere) the excuse for another long
series of adventures. But the tragic outcome of the story is
told merely as an episode, far on in the book. There had been
one more reconciliation — one more bringing back of the
vagrant wife to her vicious husband — after which the end
came quickly. For one day Mark stole up softly behind Tristram, and in Launcelot's words "the false traitor king slew
him as he sat harping before his lady la beale Isoud." There
is no sailing to Brittany: and of the poor queen's death we
are told nothing at all.

Medieval subjects, with their so-called "Gothic" exuberance
of romance, were — as Anatole France pointed out in his
otherwise unilluminating life of Jeanne d'Arc — little to the
taste of the seventeenth and eighteenth centuries. But with
the romantic revival of the nineteenth, they came again into
their own. About 1804 Sir Walter Scott edited the old British
lay of *Sir Tristrem,* which he mistakenly believed the work
of Thomas of Erceldoune: but ironically enough, it was Victorian England which saw a very renaissance of the amorous
legend. Tennyson, in his *Last Tournament,* used the story
merely as a minor episode illustrating the degradation of the
Round Table — perhaps because he had already exhausted
the theme of "faith unfaithful" in his very beautiful interpretation of Launcelot and Guinevere. While he followed
Malory's ending and Malory's characterization of Mark, his
Tristram was a lively, sensual creature who almost seemed
to evoke the contempt of Iseult herself. And as neither of
the lovers contrived to be in the least lovable or credible, the
laureate cannot be said to have added anything to the romance which had thrilled so many ages.

Swinburne, on the other hand, threw himself with characteristic fire and passion into his *Tristram of Lyonesse,* com-

ing as though in answer to his own sonorous words, to pluck

> from death of lovers dead
> Their musical soft memories, and keep red
> The rose of their remembrance in man's eyes,
> The sunsets of their stories in his skies.

The action sweeps on with a sheer ecstasy that is almost exhausting; carrying in its note of relentless fate and its frank delight in the pleasures of sense a pagan character which may be true enough to the original forms of the legend, before the Christian *jongleurs* had endeavored to baptize it. But in his prayer of the lone Iseult for Tristram —

> Nay, Lord, I pray thee let him love not me,
> Love me not any more, nor like me die,
> And be no more than such a thing as I
>
> .   .   .   .   .   .
>
> Let me die rather, and only; let me be
> Hated of him so he be loved of thee —

we are on universal ground, even close to what we like to call "holy ground" again. Swinburne's piety is, however, never so convincing as his poetry; and if the same must sometimes be admitted of those medieval minstrels who were determined to smuggle the lovers into Heaven, it is with a difference — for the medieval minstrels believed, poetically at least, in love potions, but most unquestioningly in the infinite compassion of God and the Mother of God. The really unique and memorable beauty of this version is in Swinburne's mingling of the *sea* with the lovers' story. Sailing over its sunlit waves he first pictures the young Tristram and Iseult — buried beneath its warring waves he leaves them. And when the knight lies musing just before his death, he cries out in words which seem a salty echo of Dante's Francesca da Rimini:

> Not rest but unrest hath our long love given —
> Unrest on earth that wins not rest in Heaven.
> What rest may we take ever? What have we
> Had ever more of peace than hath the sea?

There could scarcely be a sharper contrast to all this than the calm nobility of Matthew Arnold's *Tristram and Iseult.* But as the story is one not of calm but of bitter conflict he wisely confines his action to the final scene; reviving the old days of wild delight and despair only in the dreams of Tristram as he lies in the old Breton castle, waiting feverishly for the coming of "that proud, first Iseult, Cornwall's queen." She comes — bringing love and death with her: that union of love and death which were of the very essence of the magic philter, as they are the very essence of the magic music by which Richard Wagner has interpreted the story. Then Mr. Arnold transfers his interest to the widowed Iseult of Brittany, painting her with a quite unprecedented charm and sympathy, although surrounding her with a placid domesticity as unknown as it was unintended by his medieval predecessors.

After that, for almost half a century the story lay quiescent — except for the research of M. Bédier and a few other specialists — gathering momentum for the extraordinary contemporary resurgence which was to enlist the genius of Thomas Hardy, John Masefield and Edwin Arlington Robinson. An exquisite if highly expurgated prose version of the romance in the tradition of Malory but with the tenderness of Bédier, has been built up by the delicate hand of Evelyn Paul — a version scarcely to be exceeded for sheer sweetness, most piously medieval in manner if not always in matter. But the distinctly modern approach comes in the contrasting work of those three contrasting modern poets. Hardy's *Famous Tragedy of the Queen of Cornwall,* written as "a play for mummers" and printed in a limited edition in 1923, is one of the least known of his works. While most uneven in literary quality, there is a bleak beauty in its setting, a certain vividness of characterization, and real tragic intensity in the brief final scene of Tristram's murder, followed by the leap of Iseult and the devoted brachet into the sea. With its haunting prologue and epilogue spoken by Merlin, and its chorus of the shades of dead Cornish men and women, one suspects that it might endure the ordeal of actual presentation more successfully than Mr. Masefield's recent "play in verse."

For in the first place, it seems a pity that John Masefield, who writes rather uninspired drama but better narrative verse than almost any other living poet, should not have chosen the latter form for his *Tristan and Isolt.* It is regrettable, also, that he whose superlative achievement has been in poetry of ships and the sea, should have confined the action of his seafaring lovers to the land, omitting even the arresting episode of the black and white sails. In the main, however, he has held to the *letter* of romantic tradition: including the scenes of Tristan's fight with the Celtic knight, his visit to Isolt in Ireland, their drinking of the love potion with its consequences, and Mark's discovery of the sword lying between them in the forest — after which his Isolt seems to weary of Tristan and to develop a sudden loyalty to her kingly and also knightly husband. But the *spirit* of the legend he somehow fails to project; perhaps because he has tried a little too hard to be both archaic and modern, both romantic and realistic. And just as he cannot quite make up his mind whether the lovers are to invoke God or the gods, so he seems as uncertain whether they are the victims of a changeful infatuation or a grand and glamorous passion. His treatment is highly colorful and colloquial, his action almost too highly concentrated. But at least in the concluding scenes he permits a wistful beauty to surround the faulty man and woman so soon to be, in Arthur's words,

> Spirits of love, not bodies bleeding. . . .

Few, however, will care to challenge the primacy of Edwin Arlington Robinson's recent *Tristram* — not merely as one of the greatest American poems and *the* greatest yet achieved by its author, but also as the greatest recent treatment in English of its vastly poetic and popular theme. Into his blank verse narrative of medieval love and sorrow Mr. Robinson has injected the questioning introspection, the groping, the irony of an ultramodern psychology; except for a few picturesque trappings, his story might be absolutely contemporary. And to make it even more contemporary, he has — wisely or unwisely — dispensed with the love potion altogether.

> It was our curse that you were not to see
> Until you saw too late,

cries his Isolt, when immediately *after* her wedding to Mark, Tristram realizes the tragedy he could have averted; for here, as in those early French versions, it is the woman who sees first, and speaks first too. As before, Isolt of Ireland is the positive magnet of Tristram's life: Isolt of "the wild, frightened, violet eyes," magnetizing him from the safe haven of Brittany — showing him

We are not mighty enough to sentence love —
and at last, knowing when the "all" of life has passed,
reconciling her lover to death and peace.

But in trying to rationalize the passion of Tristram and
Isolt, Mr. Robinson has found that a force so consuming cannot be made rational. Also he has discovered that to make the
lovers humanly and morally responsible for all their acts,
without suggesting some form of extra-normal madness or
inebriation, increases their culpability almost to the breaking
point, if beauty is to be preserved. So in the modern pagan
fashion he reverts to some gigantic, unconquerable shadow
of Destiny — "not sin but fate" — which is probably just
what the magic philter was intended to typify from the beginning!

One has learned to expect a serious beauty and profundity
in Mr. Robinson's work — lines of a rare felicity alternating
with lines a little overweighted by words and thoughts. But
that is scarcely to be prepared for the vivid freshness of emotion he brings to the tragic story — for the ecstasy of Tristram's days at Joyous Guard, when

> He was not large enough to hold his heart,
>
> . . . . . .
>
> . And the green grass was music as he walked,

or for the almost Shakespearean music of Isolt's revery:

> Ships in their last port . . .
> have still a further voyage to make,
> Wherever it is they go. Were it not for love
> Poor life would be a ship not worth the launching.

Wisely enough, he has not been too modern to prize this
brooding music, nor to bring back the old brooding *terror*
and *pity* into his catastrophe. And *wonder,* too: the blank

wonder of unimaginative Mark — the stricken wonder of the woman who had been Tristram's negative magnet, Iseult of the White Hands, clothed with an appealing pastel beauty and left at the last groping for wisdom which, like the dawn, "comes up slowly out of an unknown ocean"; while about her are the white gulls "flying, and always flying, and still flying."

This mysterious, ever-changing immortality of the *story* down the ages is one of the things we go on taking for granted just because they go on happening — forgetting, perhaps, that the few which do achieve immortality must be capable of adapting themselves to each succeeding age. What does it matter if Tristram originally personified the Sun, and his two Iseults day and night? When the story became vital it was already intensely human — sealed indelibly by a pagan sense of Fate — gathering to itself the sometimes confused colorings of Christian chivalry — finally becoming intellectually speculative and analytical. One can never tell in which of our contemporary volumes or current magazines one will come suddenly upon the lovers, walking with as secure and as troubling a beauty as was theirs in the thirteenth century; finding them under many names, as well as under their own names. Tristram between the two Iseults — Adam between Eve and Lilith — man between the woman who represents *law* and the woman who represents *inspiration*. It is one of the oldest and most intricate problems of Life and so of the Church. Life itself has never solved it save by falling back upon Death. But the solution of the Church, looking with even eye upon Life and Death, is hinted by Patmore, the modern Catholic seer who dared to declare that "virtues are nothing but ordered passions, and vices nothing but passions in disorder."

THE LADY ANCHORESS

I T IS often difficult, of course, in studying any medieval
story, to tell where literature ends and life begins — or
where life ends and literature begins. The soap and water
of fact get themselves habitually transposed into the large
and luminous bubble of imagination. Still, there *was* this
essence of fact at the root of even the most glamorous and
extravagant bubbles. People — all kinds of people, just as
Chaucer pictures them — really did go on pilgrimages: did
they not, for better or worse, even go on crusades? Knights
really fought in tourneys, minstrels carried their treasure of
song and story from court to court, and for centuries men
and women honestly reaching out after justice believed in
the possibility of establishing truth by single combat and
even by various kinds of painful ordeals. It seems incredible;
yet something of the same belief must underlie the persistent
human resort to war — just as something of the old cruel
fallacy that human beings speak truth under torture under-
lies modern police methods.

Probably one can safely take for granted the general
background of life in any given romance; it is the details
of the story which gallop off incontinently upon the high-
road of imagination. For instance, there is the anchoress.

Fugitive references to these solitary ladies — as to the hermits
of the woods — often stray into the various romances, one of
the most piquant occurring at the end of the thirteenth and
the beginning of the fourteenth books of Malory's *Morte
d'Arthur*. Here Launcelot and Percivale, in one of the detours of the Grail quest, meet Galahad riding through a
forest, and not recognizing him, promptly draw him into
a combat in which they are both worsted. This jousting
happened, we are told, "tofore the hermitage where a recluse
dwelled." But she, no doubt drawn to her window by the
all-too-familiar sound of fighting, cries out to Galahad:
"God be with thee, best knight of the world!" — adding,
loud enough for the others to hear: "An yonder two knights
had known thee as well as I do they would not have en-
countered with thee." Thereupon Sir Galahad spurs off "at
a great pace" for fear of further recognition; while his
harassed father, riding in another direction, comes upon the
adventure of the ruined chapel, of the vision of the sick
knight healed by a visitation of the Grail — and subsequent-
ly to his own confession and shriving by a near-by hermit-
priest. But Percivale, determined to know more of the anchoress' clairvoyance, turns back to the recluse's cell and
kneeling at the window tells her his name. And the lady,
filled with great joy, commands the gates to be opened (Malory does not explain just what gates, but they were probably
those of her little garden), while the knight is offered "all
the cheer that she might make him"; for as she soon explains to Percivale: "I well ought to know you, for I am
your aunt although I be in a priory place." Then follows a
scene of deliciously domestic intimacy in which the knight,
who confesses that he has recently dreamed much about his
mother, is told of her death. His "fair aunt" comforts him

well, and she who was once Queen of the Waste Lands reveals to him Galahad's unique vocation and how Merlin
once fashioned the Round Table and the Siege Perilous:
adding for herself — "I was called the Queen of most riches
in the world; and it pleased me never my riches so much as
doth my poverty."

As usual, Malory and the earlier romancers from whom
he drew were using as a *décor* or setting the actual condi-
tions of life in the later *Moyen Age*. Dipping into that de-
lightful and scholarly summary, *Hermits and Anchorites of
England,* by Rotha Mary Clay, we find that before the six-
teenth-century cleavage English soil was fairly dotted by
recluses' cells. There were many types: solitaries of forest
and glen, light-keepers on the coast, hermits upon bridges,
and the more conservative anchorites of "church and cloister"
— among these last being many women of high birth,
particularly widows. Apparently from the beginning of the
world there have been two types of philosopher: those who
believe it is "not good for man" — still less for woman! —
"to be alone," and those who insist they are "never less alone
than when alone." The Church's answer to the spiritual individualist or solitary was the life of the hermit. And although her preference was increasingly for the safe and more
easily disciplined group of the religious community, she
provided a special office for the blessing and inclosing of anchorites; who might not enter upon their life without permission from the bishop — he, in the last resort, being responsible for their support — and who even then were generally subjected to some sort of probation. There were hun-
dreds of approved anchorages in England alone — many of
them attached to the side of a church or monastery, like the
"priory" of Percivale's aunt — evidently handed on after the

incumbent's death almost as a title to nobility. Legend linked the name of King Harold with a certain cell at Chester, declaring that after Hastings he had lived there "holily" and "made a gracious end." And there was a charming story — which Wordsworth incorporated into one of his sonnets — of how Katherine, Lady Audley (born in 1272) determined to travel on after her lord's death until she heard bells ringing without hands. This rather familiar miracle happened at the church of Ledbury, where, with her faithful maid Mabel, she remained as an anchoress until death came.

These little anchorages were generally of two rooms — although there were apparently some "duplex apartments" with two rooms on each floor, occasionally surrounded by a tiny garden. There was nearly always one window looking toward the outside, where more worldly Christians dearly loved to stop for advice or "tydings," and the most important one of all looking into the sanctuary of the adjoining church or chapel — through which the recluse might assist at Mass and other devotions, and receive Holy Communion fifteen times a year. No doubt, since we find them occasionally rebuked by their spiritual directors, some of the solitaries inclined toward excessive asceticism; but in the main an atmosphere of remarkable sweetness and sanity seems to have pervaded these anchorites' cells. "Men wit that we are in pain and penance," wrote the great mystic, Richard Rolle of Hampole, to his friend Dame Margaret: "but we have more joy in a day than they have all their life. They see our body, but they see not our heart, where is our solace." From this fourteenth-century message, as from Hilton's *Scale* or *Ladder of Perfection,* or perhaps best of all the thirteenth-century *Ancren Riwle,* it is possible to build up a very illuminating picture of the anchoress' discipline and way of life. It is a noble and serene piece of spiritual instruction, this *Regulæ Inclusarum,* generally supposed to have been written by Bishop Poore for three sisters living together as anchoresses at Tarrent in Dorsetshire. They were permitted, we find, to keep no animal but a cat — or if necessary, a cow; and much direction is given concerning that important corollary of the anchoress' life, the serving women who went in and out on needful errands. "It is very necessary for you both that you take much care of them," writes the author of the *Ancren Riwle,* "for ye may be much benefited by them; and on the other hand made worse. If they sin through your negligence ye shall be called to give account of it before the Supreme Judge. Therefore it is very necessary for you, and still more for them, that ye teach them to keep their rule . . . in a gentle manner, however, and affectionately; for such ought the instructing of women to be — affectionate and gentle, and seldom stern."

This Salesian gentleness is indeed the keynote of his work. "Do you now ask what rule you anchoresses should observe?" he continues. "Ye should by all means, with all your might and all your strength, keep well the inward rule, and for its sake the outward. The inward rule is always alike. The outward is various, because everyone ought so to observe the outward rule as that the body may therewith serve the inward. . . . My dear sisters, in like manner as ye guard well your senses externally, so above all things see that ye be gentle within; and mild and meek, affectionate and kind-hearted and patient of any word — if anyone speaks ill of you — or of any deed, if anyone harms you — lest you lose all." Every state of life has, of course, its besetting temptations, and those against which the anchoress is chiefly warned are precisely those we might expect — love of gossip

or of idleness, melancholy, and spiritual pride. "Let not anyone of remarkably pious life think that she may not be
tempted. The good, who have reached a high degree of
virtue, are more tempted than the frail . . . for the greater
and higher the hill is, there is the more wind upon it. . . .
I firmly believe that neither carnal nor spiritual temptation
shall ever master thee if thou art kind-hearted and humble
and meek, and lovest so sincerely all men and women, and
especially anchoresses, that thou art as sorry for their evil
and glad of their good as of thine own." Then Bishop Poore,
or whoever it was who wrote these golden words, breaks
into a striking metaphor: "If the chalice could speak, which
was molten in the fire and made to boil vehemently, and
then with much beating and polishing made into so very
beautiful a form for the service of God, would it curse the
purifying fire and the hands of its artificer? The whole
world is God's smithy, in which He forgeth His elect.
Wouldst thou that God had no fire in His smithy, nor bel-
lows, nor hammers?" . . . And the volume ends with the
naïve plea: "As often as ye read anything in this book, greet
the Lady with an Ave Mary for him who made this rule,
and for him who wrote it and took pains about it. Moderate
enough I am, who ask so little."

But what was to be the flower, the fruit, of all this intensive gardening? What, besides good advice, did the anchoress
give to the world she had forsaken? It is interesting to remember how the thirteenth-century Belgian recluse, Eve,
sheltered in her cell St. Juliana of Liège when the latter was
driven from her convent, both sharing and encouraging the
efforts by which that valiant Benedictine was largely responsible for introducing — or shall one say, for imploring? —
the joyous feast of Corpus Christi into the Church. But pos-

sibly the spiritual achievement may best be gauged by its
high-water mark in the highly personal work of another
Juliana, the *Revelations* of that true and tender mystic
known as Blessed Julian of Norwich. We know rather little
externally about this remarkable woman except that she occupied an anchorage at the east end of the old Norman
church at Norwich, that she was probably of noble birth,
and possibly educated at the near-by Benedictine convent of
Carrow; where, in spite of the fact that she habitually speaks
of herself as "a simple creature, unlettered," she may or may
not have taken vows as a Benedictine nun. Clearly she possessed a fine and well-trained mind, capable of drawing delicate distinctions in theology and psychology, along with a
heart full of compassion and fellowship toward our faulty
world and a soul absorbed in devotion to God and fealty to
the Catholic faith. It was during the May of 1373 when she
was "thirty years old and a half," and transported by the
combination of severe physical illness and spiritual ardor
into a psychic state in which she at first thought her soul
had really left her body in death, that there were revealed to
her fifteen distinct "Shewings" or "Revelations" of God's
love. Afterwards, as pain again submerged body and mind,
came a reaction of doubt, almost of despair. Then on the
following night was granted the Sixteenth Revelation, a
confirmation of all the others. And the rest of Lady Julian's
life — she was "esteemed one of the greatest holiness" in
1393 and seems to have lived on until 1413 — was spent in
meditating upon the message of "wisdom and truth and
love," and in expounding it for the consolation of her "even-
Christians." For this woman, who had separated herself
from everyday life, was singularly untouched by Pharisaism.
"Because of the Shewing I am not good but if I love God

the better," she writes. "For I am certain that there be many that never had Shewing nor Sight but of the common teaching of Holy Church, that love God better than I." And her immediate impulse after that first revelation was to be "greatly stirred in charity to mine even-Christians, that they might see and know the same that I saw: for I would it were comfort to them." Comfort, indeed, it must have been for the fellow-Christians of her own day — and may well be for her fellow-Christians today — to realize vividly the "courtesy," the "marvelous homeliness" of God to man, His tender, brooding care, the "goodness which cometh down to the lowest part of our need," His unfailing Light and Life and Love.

Julian's revelations seem to have had two sides; a concrete *vision* and an abstract *teaching* — similar to the familiar "preludes" and "considerations" still recommended for meditation or mental prayer. The visions represented for the most part some phase of Christ's Passion upon which the anchoress was accustomed to meditate, such as the Crowning with Thorns, the Scourging, the Paling of the Face in Death. She had "Shewing" also of Our Lady, first as "a simple maid and meek, in the stature that she was when she conceived," later in her exalted "truth, her wisdom, her charity"; after which Christ asks: *"Wilt thou see in her how thou art loved? For thy love I made her so high, so noble, so worthy."* Equally comforting and characteristic is this little colloquy following the Passion scenes: *"Art thou well pleased that I suffered for thee?* I said, Yea, good Lord, I thank Thee; yea, good Lord, blessed mayst Thou be. Then said Jesus, our Kind Lord: *If thou art pleased I am pleased; it is a joy, a bliss, an endless satisfying to me that ever suffered I Passion for thee; and if I might suffer more, I would suffer more."* And Julian understands that "the love that made Him to suffer passeth so far all His Passion as Heaven is above Earth." Soon afterward the anchoress finds herself transported from great "sureness" and joy to depths of spiritual desolation and weariness where scarcely she can "have patience to live" — in order that she may realize how "He keepeth us even alike secure in woe and weal." Then, in the exquisite Sixth Revelation, there is sounded a note of consoling beauty not too common even in the most beautiful of spiritual writings. For Julian sees her Lord reigning as it were in His own house, "fulfilling it with joy and mirth," welcoming His "dearworthy friends," and giving to her own humility the tremendous message: *"I thank thee for thy travail, and especially for thy youth."*

There is more than one revelation from which all sensuous and emotional matter is eliminated. "After this I saw God in a point, that is to saẏ, in mine understanding — by which sight I saw that He is in all things." But seeing this, Julian goes further, asking herself the immemorial question, *What is sin?* And the remainder of this Shewing, with the whole of the Thirteenth, are concerned with this question, never fully explained nor perhaps explainable to our human intelligence. For, like all sensitive souls tormented by the incomprehensible evil of the world, she wonders "Why, by the great foreseeing wisdom of God, the beginning of sin was not hindered?" In many of her conclusions Julian is charmingly childlike and ingenuous, but there is no *naïveté* in her treatment of this problem: her bewilderment is the bewilderment of poets and philosophers and theologians down all the ages. Sin, she perceives, is "the sharpest scourge that any chosen soul may be smitten with" — yet, meditating upon the eternal, positive realities, she is tempted to believe that it "hath no manner of substance . . . nor could it be known but by the pain it is cause of." This fourteenth-century English-woman, like the poet of thirteenth-century Florence, desires that she may have "full sight of Hell and Purgatory"; but it is characteristic that her imagination, attuned to mercy rather than to justice, finds it utterly impossible to conceive his tragic and sinister depths. What she is given to understand is a series of intensely practical and comforting conclusions: that she must see her own sins rather than other people's — that she and everybody else must follow the triune guide of *natural reason, the common teaching of Holy Church, and the inward, gracious working of the Holy Ghost* — that both "in falling and in rising we are ever preciously kept in one love" — and that He would have us be patient with ourselves and all other sinners, living "gladly and merrily, for His love," even in our penance. For the rest, she is taught as was Dante that there are two parts of Truth: the one, concerning our salvation, which is "clear and fair and light" — the other which is of "our Lord's privy counsel," not to be revealed in this life. But with this reservation comes the trumpetlike promise of God: *"It is sooth that sin is the cause of all this pain; but all shall be well . . . I may make all things well . . . I shall make all things well . . . And thou shalt see thyself that all manner of thing shall be well."*

Dame Julian's teaching about prayer, the Fourteenth Revelation, is of most exalted spirituality — but it will not be of much comfort to those of us who would be too *particular* in our supplications. "This," she declares, "is our Lord's will, that our prayer and our trust be both alike large"; and if after long prayer we have not our asking, she is confident that "either we abide a better time, or more grace, or a better gift." After all, she seems to say, what does it matter? The *greatest deeds* — our Creation, our Redemption, the ordering of Faith and of Nature — are *already* done: we have but to bring ourselves into harmony with God's will to attain His bliss. *"Prayer oneth the soul to God."* She would have us realize that this union is its glory and its chief end. There is the simplicity of genius also in her words upon the mystery of Death. "It is the more blissful that man be taken from pain, than that pain be taken from man," she cries; telling her vision of the prostrate, shapeless body lying upon the earth, from which sprang suddenly "a full fair creature, a little child . . . nimble and lively, whiter than a lily," returning where there shall be "no manner of pain, no manner of misliking, no wanting of will" . . . only God!

It seems curious, but after all it is frightfully human, that after having soared so high Julian should have been temporarily cast down again to the depths, as she herself puts it, of "feebleness, wretchedness and blindness." At the beginning of those fifteen mysterious Revelations, she tells us how all the long pain of her illness was suddenly taken away; at their close it seems to have returned with renewed agony, and for a few hours the weak body so prevailed over the strong spirit that she not only doubted the reality of her visions but was even swept into a nightmare dream (she is careful to tell us the heavenly "Shewings" never came in sleep) of being overcome by the Fiend or Satan himself. Then "our courteous Lord gave me grace to waken . . . and I was brought to great rest and peace, without sickness of body or dread of conscience." During the next night "our Lord opened my spiritual eye and shewed me my soul in midst of my heart" — with God, "clad majestically," sitting as king in this soul. And it was, says the anchoress, a singular joy and bliss that she saw Him sitting rather than standing; "for the secureness of sitting sheweth endless dwelling." As on the first Pentecost the Paraclete came to the Apostles, "teaching them and bringing all things to their remembrance," so now the "good Lord" comforts this devoted woman, assuring her that the former visions were true, explaining their meaning, and promising her the grace of final perseverance. "He said not: *Thou shalt not be tempested, thou shalt not be travailed, thou shalt not be afflicted;* but He said, *Thou shalt not be overcome.* . . . And soon after, all was close and I saw no more. . . ."

There were to be no more visions in Julian's life — and indeed, no more were needed. She had sought and found the "one thing needful," and had but to savor it, to absorb its beauty as one absorbs the beauty of a rose or of a jewel, for her own enrichment and that of her "even-Christians." Also, and in spite of what a sophisticated critic might incline to call sentimentality, this anchoress of Norwich attained rare balance; for if on one hand she perceived God as Father and Mother and Spouse — as Trinity and Unity and "endless fulfilling of all true desires" — on the other she was never weary of insisting that "though we be highly lifted up into contemplation," it is none the less necessary to keep "meek remembrance of our frailties" and firm hold upon the Church and her Sacraments.

But it is the very nature of a revelation that it shall be *particular* — coming to a particular soul and teaching a particular lesson. And even as the stars, one revelation differs from another in glory. For fifteen years Julian meditated upon the special reason and interpretation of the Shewings once granted to her. Finally she was answered "in ghostly understanding: *Wouldst thou learn thy Lord's meaning in* *this thing? Learn it well: Love was His meaning. Who shewed it thee? Love. What shewed He thee? Love. Wherefore shewed it He? For love. Thou shalt never know nor learn therein other thing without end."** After all, it was matter enough for one little book, or one little life!

The anchoress has gone from us, it seems. She has no place in our modern world and is scarcely remembered in our modern literature. Miss Willa Cather does, indeed, point out the shadow of the saintly recluse of seventeenth-century Montreal. But there is something a little frigid and formidable in that indomitable young Canadian girl who hid herself away to converse with the angels. The medieval anchoress did not scorn to talk familiarly through her little window with the men and women passing by. She seemed less like an exotic than a fragrant and friendly perennial. And the message she has handed down for our comfort may well be that simple, universal sentence of the *Ancren Riwle* — "Nothing is ever so hard that love doth not make it tender and sweet."

Revelations of Divine Love. Recorded by Julian, Anchoress at Norwich, a version from the MS. in the British Museum, edited by Grace Warrack. Methuen and Co., Ltd.

A MEDIEVAL WORLDLING:
ELEANOR OF AQUITAINE

IF THERE is one thing we moderns are always striving for and priding ourselves upon it is inclusiveness — our synthesis of the arts, the far sweep of our science and our psychology, in general the "infinite variety" of our approach to life. But it was our medieval ancestors who really sucked their orange dry; who between two good things always, like the fabled optimist, chose both — often adding a few evil things for good measure. The Middle Ages have suffered much, first from defamation, then over-idealization. They were the centuries when the broken and rusty civilizations of Greece and Rome and the young barbarisms of Europe were being put into the melting pot, forged, gradually wrought into the new civilizations of Christendom. Only it is just as well to remember that no civilization has ever been entirely Christian, that no civilization has ever been entirely civilized. Human beings since Eden, even since Calvary, are what they are — sometimes a little better, sometimes a little worse. And the Middle Ages, particularly the later Middle Ages, being a time of superabundant vitality, gave us great thinkers, great builders, great fighters, great saints, and if one may so express it, great sinners. And between the hills of the saints and the valleys of the sinners stretches always the immense, slanting middle ground — No Man's Land, Every Man's Land — of the worldlings, with limitless possibilities for climbing and for slipping back.

The medieval worldling, in whom the good seed of the Faith once sown was choked by the cares and riches and pleasures of this life, has perhaps not been sufficiently recognized. Many men, many women, might be singled out as examples — but somehow the best way to study *him* in the abstract seems to be to study *her* in the concrete. Personally, I can think of few women more absolutely concrete or vivid or worldly than Eleanor of Aquitaine, queen first of France then of England, who would have been what the French call a *maitresse femme* in any age. Eleanor, or Eléonore or Aliénor, was born probably in the year 1122, daughter of the powerful Duke William X of Aquitaine — who died at Compostello on the Good Friday of 1137, while seeking to do penance for a fairly faulty life — and granddaughter of the celebrated crusading troubadour, William IX. Legend has handed down the story of a mysterious pilgrim who faced her far-from-immaculate father and mother a few days before Eleanor's birth with the prophecy: *De vous il ne sortira rien de bon.* But nobody ever seems to have been deterred from anything by unpleasant prophecies; and shortly after her father's death the young duchess was wedded, as he had arranged, to the neighboring Prince Louis of France. A month later the eighteen-year-old groom, his kingdom vastly stretched by the immense dowry of Aquitaine — including Guyenne, Poitou, Limousin, Gascony, and in fact all of France between the Pyrennees, the Ocean, and the river Garonne — brought by his fifteen-year-old bride, became king as Louis VII.

Long before this Eleanor had reigned as uncrowned queen

of her father's Provençal duchy, surrounded by the best poets and minstrels of her time. Hers was the age and home of that curious medieval creation, the Court of Love; and over these literary and amorous competitions the beautiful, frivolous Eleanor — with her sister the beautiful and frivolous Petronilla — queened it royally. Few things could better illustrate that unconscious inclusiveness of medieval life than the fact that both anchoress and Court of Love should have thriven at the same time. They were the two polar extremes, between which lay the more normal developments of everyday life in home or cloister. From such universally translated works as the Tristram romances or the *Romaunt of the Rose,* from the exquisite twelfth-century *chante-fable* of *Aucassin and Nicolette,* or the heart-shaking poignancy of the thirteenth-century *Vita Nuova,* we see how increasingly medieval poets insisted upon the sacrosanct importance of love between man and woman. Indeed they made of it first a cult, then a convention. This gradual exaltation or spiritualization of romantic love was at root the challenge of a Christian sacrament and a Christian civilization to the old, frankly physical love of paganism; and Dante's praise of his idolized Beatrice is at once so like and so unlike Patmore's praise of his wedded Emily that it is interesting to compare them. To the Florentine poet his beloved seems *"not a woman but one of the beautiful angels of Heaven"* — to the Victorian she is *"The Angel in the House."* But there were conventions of this *amour courtois* which tended to become highly artificial and even highly anarchic — as for instance that the lady must be maritally unattainable, and addressed under a wealth of subterfuge and euphemism which would drive her modern sisters to distraction. Naturally enough, and fortunately enough in a world where might still ruled, this whole idea of romantic love was soon linked up with the etiquette of Chivalry; so that the defense of all helpless womanhood and the devout service of one symbolic woman became the duty of every true knight. Then most unfortunately, it got itself entangled with poetic excesses and eventually with the Manichean heresies of that luxurious land of Provence which gave birth not only to the troubadours but also to the Albigenses.

Overwhelmingly lovely Eleanor must have been, and overwhelmingly lovable in the physical sense at least. But there has rarely been a woman so heartily hated by her contemporaries — with the exception of the poets, who, from Peyrols to Bernard de Ventadour, were usually on her side. "Serpent" was her mildest sobriquet, and she seems to have been blamed for nearly all of her various families' misdemeanors. When, for instance, King Louis was at war with Champagne, she was held responsible for the tragic suggestion to fire certain houses in the town of Vitry — from which the flames spread to the cathedral, destroying some thirteen hundred people who had there sought sanctuary. This act brought a prompt interdict from the Pope; and Louis, overwhelmed with remorse, volunteered enthusiastically by way of expiation when Bernard of Clairvaux came preaching the Second Crusade in 1146. Eleanor, always a lover of adventure, volunteered also, bringing with her a picturesque regiment of ladies-in-waiting; and her willfulness and wantonness seem to have contributed not a little to the failure of the whole sad enterprise. Possibly she was not guilty of an intrigue with the boyish Saladin in the Holy Land; possibly her insistence upon camping outside of orders was not responsible for the defeat of her husband's army near Laodicea. But both charges have been handed down, and there is little doubt that she became involved in a rather serious scandal with her hand-some kinsman, Raymond of Antioch. Eleanor, with her in-flammable Midi temperament, was the last type to resist the all-too-easy deterioration of the West in contact with the burning East, and Louis brought her back to France in sorrow and disgust. Three years later — in 1152 — both seem to have been delighted when the local council of Beaugency consented to dissolve their marriage on grounds of cousin-ship.

The occasional intrusion of these royal annulments during the Middle Ages — for reasons of consanguinity, lack of con-sent, or some minor impediment which could easily have been obviated before the ceremony — undoubtedly raises the question of abuse. But the abuse was far more frequently on the civil than on the ecclesiastical side. Willful and imper-fect men and women, faced by a perfect and often sacrificial ideal of monogamy, sought then as they seek now for means of evasion. Divorce was not yet considered a solution by even nominal Christians: but there is reason to suspect that in more than one royal marriage some not-impossible flaw — like the failure to secure a valid dispensation — was deliber-ately permitted for state reasons. For in every generation the "children of this world" are at least superficially wiser than the "children of light."

At any rate, Eleanor was no sooner free than almost every eligible prince set out to capture her: for was she not one of the greatest heiresses and most beautiful princesses in Europe? Her own preference went to Henry Plantagenet, eleven years her junior but heir, through his mother Matilda, to the English throne. To him she offered herself and her dowry — both being accepted with alacrity. And two years later, in 1154, she found herself crowned queen-consort of

England. There was some fighting between the former husband, Louis VII, and the new husband, Henry II; as the
French King had naturally enough expected the dowry of
Aquitaine to descend to Marie and Alix, his daughters by
Eleanor. But as usual the imperious lady had her way, taking
her counties across the Channel with her and so planting
the seeds of that century-long conflict between France and
England which Jeanne d'Arc was eventually and triumph-
antly to solve.

In England the presence of a Provençal queen gave strong
impetus to lyric poetry as well as to the Continental romance.
"Thanks to the first, then to the second marriage of the
Duchess of Guyenne, the peculiar art which, from the Limousin, had rapidly spread over the south, penetrated northern France," writes Gaston Paris. "She diffused the doctrines
of 'courtois' love and the art which expressed them through
the courts of France and England. In their turn, the two
daughters she had by Louis VII, above all the Countess Marie
of Champagne, cultivated them with ardor; the sons she had
by Henry II, Henry 'the young king,' Geoffrey of Brittany
and Richard, loved and encouraged poetry, and served as in-
termediaries between that of the North and that of the
South."* But ironically enough, destiny was to brand Eleanor
not friend but enemy of romantic love, through her persecu-
tion — possibly even her murder — of "fair Rosamond."
Henry Plantagenet was a man of action rather than of sen-
timent or emotion, a man of little faith and few scruples, yet
capable enough in bringing law and order out of the anarchy
of Stephen's reign. And by another ironical paradox, the most
amiable episode of his whole stormy life seems to have been

Mediaeval French Literature.

his devotion to the gentle Rosamond de Clifford. Some chroniclers assert that he had met "fair Rosamond" during one of his youthful visits to England, and had planned to make her his queen until the opportunity to wed Eleanor of Aquitaine switched him from love to ambition. Still others declare that she knew the king only by one of his minor titles and believed herself his wife; that she lived in seclusion at Woodstock and bore Henry two sons whom he later publicly recognized — the Geoffrey who eventually became Archbishop of York and the William, Earl of Salisbury, to be known as "Longsword." Since in such meticulous records as the *Dictionary of National Biography** scarcely a date or fact of Rosamond's life is left uncontested — except, indeed, her noble birth, her liaison with King Henry, and her burial at Godstow Abbey — and since her story has become one of the recognized sources of English romance, one may claim poetic license to choose the most fitting and romantic traditions available. Fabyan's *Chronicle* gives the familiar tale of the mazelike house and of the silken thread attached to Henry's spur by which Eleanor tracked her rival, much as in Masefield's recent poem, adding: "The common fame tellyth that lastly the queen wone to her . . . and delte with her in such maner that she lyved not long after." Whether this dealing was in bitter word or more bitter work we are left to surmise, for there is no reference as yet to the dagger or poison of the seventeenth-century ballad quoted by Bishop Percy. But there is a distinct legend that Rosamond's elaborate tomb before the altar of Godstow Abbey (a nunnery largely endowed by her father, Walter de Clifford), later gave scandal to St. Hugh of Lincoln, who ordered it dis-

*Q. v. *Rosamond de Clifford.*

mantled and the unhappy lady's body buried outside the chapel.

Queen Eleanor, during the course of her second marriage, bore Henry five sons and three daughters — and while never a very satisfactory wife, she seems to have been a capable and devoted mother. She was back pacifying her own Guyenne, which she had determined should be under young Richard's rule, when in 1170 Thomas à Becket was assassinated before the altar at Canterbury. A gasp of horror swept across England when the murder of the heroic primate, champion of Church rights against the encroaching State, became known. King Henry, recognized as morally responsible for the act and threatened both by papal excommunication and the desertion of his realm, dropped the attempted conquest of Ireland and all his other wars to walk barefoot to the martyr's shrine and submit to the penance of a public flagellation by the seventy monks of the Cathedral chapter. Meanwhile his "hated queen" — whether before or after the Rosamond episode is not clear — certainly aided if she did not inspire the great rebellion of her sons against their father in 1173. And being captured while trying to escape to France in man's attire, she was imprisoned — or as we might say, interned — for the rest of her kingly husband's life. It is said that the young Prince Henry, whom she had hoped to see upon the throne in his father's place, pleaded for Eleanor unavailingly before his death in 1183. Six years later Henry II, worn by wars and family feuds and driven even from his native Le Mans, went sullenly to the last Home of all. One hopes the story of his dying blasphemies, handed down by Gerald de Barri, is not true — just as one hopes the account of the patient death-bed devotion of the pious but illegitimate son, Geoffrey, may have some foundation in fact.

At any rate, freedom came now to Eleanor, and she used it well: making a royal progress through England, freeing political prisoners, reconciling the turbulent lords and by sheer force of her own character securing the succession for Richard, "the Lion-Hearted."* During his subsequent imprisonment after the Third Crusade it was his queen-mother and regent — then seventy years of age — who crushed the rebellion of her youngest son John, took possession of Wallingford and Windsor Castles, and with the help of Herbert Walter, the able Archbishop of Canterbury, raised and despatched Richard's enormous ransom in 1193. She knew and despised John's perfidy, but with a characteristic blending of maternal loyalty and ambition she fought again indomitably until she secured his coronation when Richard himself died in 1199.

Perhaps it may be counted as a little righteousness to Eleanor that one of her last diplomatic acts was a visit to Castile to arrange the marriage of her granddaughter Blanche to young Louis, the grandson of Louis VII — from which union was to be born the saint-king, Louis IX. Nothing except Death could still her activities, but at last, in 1204, he had his way; and the woman who had summed up so much of the history of her time was laid quietly to sleep in the Angevin Abbey of Fontevrault. In many senses her passing marked the close of an era — a particularly worldly, turbulent and defiant era, which came near bringing the cataclysm of the Reformation some three hundred years before its appointed time. Not a few in the so-called Dark Ages had believed that the end of the world, the *millennium,* was to

*For many authoritative details of the lives of Eleanor and Henry II, see the *Dictionary of National Biography.*

come in the year 1000: when it failed to arrive, there was a
good deal of confusion, a let-down in austerity and a general weakening of that "blind" and childlike faith which
was soon to give place to the highly intelligent, analytical
faith of a Dante or a Thomas Aquinas. It was one of the
periodical intervals when, as Mr. Chesterton puts it, "The
Church looked old . . . and there were some who thought
her dying then as now."* To the contemporary poet Peyrols, seeing the work of the Crusades undone and Jerusalem
crushed again under Moslem rule while the Christian monarchs, Richard, Philip Augustus, and Frederick, bickered before her gates, it might well seem that the whole world was
"going down in decadence."*

But the colossal Christian creativeness of the thirteenth and
fourteenth centuries was at hand, and already the reaction
had set in. Over in Umbria, young Francis Bernardone was
beginning to sing and to act his praise of Humility, of Love,
of the Lady Poverty. In the diocese of Toulouse, the very
year after Eleanor's death, the burning beacon of Saint Dominic had drawn so many feminine converts back to the
Church — women being always prime supporters of Albi-
gensianism, as of the later Christian Science which in many
ways resembles it — that a convent had to be built for them.
And in 1209 he was commissioned by Pope Innocent III to
preach the final crushing crusade against that heresy.
Whether Queen Eleanor herself was tainted by the unlovely
Neo-Manichean doctrines so popular in her beloved Provence
it would be difficult to prove. Abstract ideas seem to have interested her about as little as they interested Queen Eliza-

St. Francis of Assisi.
Grand Dictionnaire Larousse: Peyrols of Auvergne.

beth, unless they could be twisted into some concrete personal or dynastic advantage. She was the typical worldling — the individualist born several centuries too late or too early: like Bernard Shaw's millionaire, she was of those who believe chiefly in *themselves*.

In this sense there is something strikingly modern in Eleanor's attitude toward society and the Church. It is difficult to remember that her son John was to be forced to sign the Magna Charta of England — that her granddaughter Blanche was to build the Cathedral of Chartres — that the Dominican and Franciscan friars she would probably have despised were to bring back to the Church that perennial "Miracle of Resurrection" to which, as Robert Hugh Benson pointed out, "she has always appealed, and which has never failed her yet."* But perhaps most difficult of all is it to realize that Eleanor's ruthless, sensual sophistication was two full centuries younger than the divine simplicity of Jeanne d'Arc, who was to undo her work politically, patriotically — as love goes on undoing the work of hate — as the Blessed Virgin goes on undoing the work of Eve.

*Christ in the Church.

THE PILGRIM'S PROGRESS AND SOME
PRE-REFORMATION ALLEGORIES

WHEN, a little more than fifty years ago, M. Taine wrote his *History of English Literature,* he made bold to assert that "After the Bible, the book most widely read in England is the *Pilgrim's Progress,* by John Bunyan." That was a judgment from without the gates, and its accuracy may have been questionable; but it has its value as an impression, none the less. For today, not even a French critic would dream of repeating the statement! The sway of this quaint Puritan epic has quite manifestly waned at last: it has migrated from the realm of living and influencing books into the realm of literary curiosities. Yet once upon a time Bunyan's masterpiece was, in all truth, a manual of popular devotion — a Protestant *Imitation* ever at hand for the admonition of childhood and the edification of old age. It is amazing how many household words and household thoughts the "Dream" of this great, illiterate man has furnished us. Vanity Fair, the Slough of Despond, Mercy's Dream, the Man with the Muck Rake, the Valley of Humiliation, the Delectable Mountains — these have passed into the common heritage of English-speaking men and women, to remain upon the lips of thousands who may never have opened the volume which gave them birth.

Bunyan himself, one need scarcely state, was a tinker and later a Nonconformist preacher of Bedford, England. His chief work — *The Pilgrim's Progress from This World to That Which Is to Come, Delivered Under the Similitude of a Dream, et cetera, et cetera* — was almost certainly composed during a six months' imprisonment for Dissentient preaching in 1675;* and not during that earlier incarceration of twelve years (1660–72) for the same cause. If we may accept Bunyan's very naïve account, the masterpiece was achieved somewhat in spite of himself. He had no intention of making "a little book in such a mode"; in fact, he was engaged upon a wholly different volume: but the Muse was importunate and would not be denied.

> And thus it was: I writing of the way
> And race of Saints in this our gospel day,
> Fell suddenly into an allegory
> About their journey and the way to glory,
> In more than twenty things which I set down.
> This done, I twenty more had in my crown;
> And they again began to multiply
> Like sparks that from the coals of fire do fly. . . .

At last, fearing lest this fruitful similitude should quite "eat out" the substance of his original work, Bunyan permitted it to creep into a separate volume — and *The Pilgrim's Progress* had won its right to live! His Puritan friends seem to have disagreed concerning the wisdom of publishing so ingenious a fantasy:

> Some said, John, print it; others said, Not so:
> Some said, It might do good; others said, No.

*Cf. *The Pilgrim's Progress as John Bunyan Wrote It.* Introduction by John Brown.

In which quandary John, very sensibly, decided the case for himself, placing his manuscript in the hands of one Nath. Ponder, at the Peacock, in the Poultry near Cornhill. The first edition of his work appeared in 1678, and met with overwhelming success. A second and enlarged edition was put forth the same year; and the complete work as we now know it was published in the third edition of 1679.

The story will perhaps bear a brief repetition. Bunyan, walking through the wilderness of this world, lighted upon a place where there was a Den (so he denominates the Town Gaol on Bedford Bridge!) and lying down to sleep, he dreamed:

"And behold, I saw a man clothed with rags, standing in a certain place, with his face from his own house, a book in his hand, and a great burden upon his back. I looked, and saw him open the book, and read therein; and as he read, he wept and trembled; and not being able longer to contain, he brake out with a lamentable cry, saying, *What shall I do?*"

It is Christian, loaded with his sins, and longing to flee away from the City of Destruction. His wife has little but contempt for these disquieting aspirations; and Christian is well-nigh in despair for lack of guidance, when upon a day Evangelist appears before him, bearing a scroll with the words, *Flee from the wrath to come.* Bunyan's description of their interview is austerely eloquent:

"The man therefore read it and looking upon Evangelist very carefully said: Whither must I fly? Then said Evangelist, pointing with his finger over a very wide field: Do you see yonder wicket-gate? The man said: No. Then said the other: Do you see yonder shining light? He said: I think I do. Then said Evangelist: Keep that light in your eye and go up directly thereto; so shalt thou see the gate; at which when thou knockest, it shall be told thee what thou shalt do. So I saw in my dream that the man began to run. Now, he had not run far from his own door, but his wife and children, perceiving it, began to cry after him to return; but the man put his fingers in his ears, and ran on crying: Life! life! Eternal life! So he looked not behind him, but fled towards the middle of the plain."

We are at once in the thick of the allegory, and Bunyan's copious marginal notes permit no doubt as to the particular moral he would enforce. There is scarcely a paragraph, moreover, without abundant and more or less apposite allusions to Scriptural texts. No less than six of these references adorn (?) the brief passage quoted above: indeed this literal and minute Bibliolatry is exceedingly characteristic of Bunyan's temper, and colors at every turn his literary work. It is in his minor characters, not his heroic types, that we recognize a veritable, if one-sided, humanity. For they, having but a single moral to point, do this vigorously enough by simply being themselves. And more than once they prove the Puritan preacher a keen, practical observer of middle-class English life — no mean prophet, in fact, of the coming realism of Defoe. Hopeful, with his little fugitive frailties, is a more appealing figure than the central Pilgrim. And in very spite of himself Bunyan has invested Ignorance with a humanity not to be despised — that humanity which reaches its climax when he flatly refuses to believe his heart as evil as Christian declares its natural state to be! There is more than a touch of the old imperishable romances, too, in the adventures of our Pilgrim — although he stands from first to last a type of Puritan righteousness. Christian faces his den of lions in splendid ignorance of their detaining chains; he falls into slumber in a certain pleasant arbor — and loses his passport scroll; he is taken prisoner, only to escape at great hazard from Doubting Castle. His battle with the fiend, Apollyon, is almost worthy of Malory, or the *Legend of St. Margaret.*

"In this combat," writes Bunyan, "no one can imagine, unless he had seen and heard as I did, what yelling and hideous roaring Apollyon made all the time of the fight." At one crisis, breaking out into a grievous rage at Christian's defiance, he "straddled quite over the whole breadth of the way, and said: I am void of fear in this matter; prepare thyself to die; for I swear by my infernal den that thou shalt go no further; here will I spill thy soul. And with that he threw a flaming dart at his breast; but Christian had a shield in his hand with which he caught it, and so prevented the danger of that."

More than half a day this "sore combat" endured, Apollyon's darts flying as thick as hail, the pilgrim defending himself, although hard spent, and wounded in head and hand and foot. At the last he regains his sword and strikes the fiend a telling blow. "And with that Apollyon spread forth his dragon's wings, and sped him away, that Christian for a season saw him no more."

It is small wonder that generations of pious readers, nourished in a bare and unlovely faith, have rejoiced in this spirited allegory of their pilgrimage! It is still less surprising that little children — who knew not Godfrey and the Crusaders, nor Roland nor Arthur! — have hung spellbound over the adventures of this sober Christian knight. Moreover, there are friendly castles and friendly greetings upon the pilgrim's way; although Christian has yet to cross the Enchanted Ground, and the Valley of the Shadow of Death, with its snares and pitfalls. Perhaps his most *human,* his most universal moment occurs at the final ordeal when, sinking in the deep waters, he cries aloud for help:

"Ah my friend, 'the sorrows of death have compassed me about'; I shall not see the land that flows with milk and honey; and with that a great darkness and horror fell upon Christian, so that he could not see before him. Also here he in great measure lost his senses, so that he could neither remember nor orderly talk of any of those sweet refreshments that he had met with in the way of his pilgrimage."

But it is quickly over; and Christian with his companion Hopeful, are welcomed by a host of Shining Men and led to the gate of the Celestial City. Bunyan's eyes are loath to lose sight of his pilgrims. He sees them transfigured and clothed in shining raiment, while the bells of the city ring for joy; and then at last:

"Just as the gates were opened to let in the men, I looked in after them, and behold, the city shone like the sun; the streets also were paved with gold, and in them walked many men, with crowns on their heads, palms in their hands, and golden harps to sing praises withal. There were also of them that had wings, and they answered one another without intermission, saying: 'Holy, holy, holy is the Lord!' And after that they shut up the gates; which, when I had seen, I wished myself among them. . . . So I awoke, and behold it was a dream."

The Second Part of the *Pilgrim's Progress* — Bunyan's somewhat tardy apotheosis of the spiritual life of woman — lacks both the vigor and the inspiration of Christian's story. Like most sequels, it is often hard put to maintain the spirit of its predecessor. Sadly indeed must the narrative have halted but for Great Heart's timely advent; for neither in

Mercy nor Christiana (poor, amiable, edifying wraiths of womanhood!) is there vitality enough to support a decent allegory. The incidental verses, too, with the exception of one charming *Shepherd's Song,* are particularly infelicitous: so that one suspects those generously interspersed sermons of having exhausted Bunyan's creative faculties — as more than once they threaten to exhaust his readers' much-tried patience. If there be one possible gain over Part First, it is the author's gain in charity; for he who consigned Ignorance straight to hell at the beatific close of his earlier vision, narrates in this latter God's gracious acceptance of Feeble Mind and Ready-to-Halt, of Mr. Despondency and his daughter Much Afraid.

There is, of course, nothing very subtle in this allegory of life. Its types are obvious enough; and if Bunyan writes with a sturdy eloquence, at moments not unfired by poetry nor unlightened by humor, his appeal is always — and essentially — to mediocrity. He was a great popular preacher, and he became a phenomenally popular writer; but he was never at any moment prophet or mystic. In what, then, lies the excellence of this *Pilgrim's Progress* — the secret of its enduring vitality and fascination? No doubt a very simple fact must explain. The book tells a great, elemental story — the story of man's struggling and aspiring soul — in the words and scenes of everyday life. There is the abstract, the universal type, Christian; laboring through the Slough of Despond and the Valley of Humiliation, fighting demons, outwitting Giant Despair, resting upon the Delectable Mountains, and passing at last through the choking waters of Death. But crossing the path of this Pilgrim come Obstinate and Pliable, whom we all have known; Mr. Worldly Wiseman, and Talkative, smooth and satisfied in his airy loquacity. It is all as colloquial as possible: and yet at bottom it is essentially, eternally poetic. For in his Bible Bunyan found matter of high and sublime poetry — matter upon which his own allegory was often but a homely, running comment.

From his forced and sometimes violent introduction of texts, may one not perceive what awesome things lay struggling in his thought? The Ditch into which the Blind have led the Blind in all ages — the Highway of Righteousness and the Very Narrow Gate — the Valley of the Shadow of Death, and not less the River of the Water of Life. . . . At moments, recalling the rich creative freedom, the mystical and flamelike soaring of our medieval allegorists, we are tempted to demand whether this close adherence to the letter of the Scriptures may not have warped and stereotyped Bunyan's imagination. Far more truly it created it! For without that long and solitary and impassioned meditation upon his Bible, I believe the Bedford preacher had never been a poet at all.

In the light of present-day vagaries, the Catholic reader is often surprised to note the orthodoxy of these seventeenth-century Dissenters — their hold upon Christ, upon the Holy Trinity, and many cardinal points of faith. Yet the reigning theology of the *Pilgrim's Progress* is, of course, a Protestant theology. Throughout Bunyan's entire work there is no mention of the sacraments: there is even the strangest and most pervasive Hebraism. For, in truth, they were "Old Testament Christians" — these brave-hearted and narrow-minded Puritans for whom he wrote — far more interested in Jacob's ladder, Moses' rod, "the pitchers, trumpets, and lamps, too, with which Gideon put to flight the armies of Midian,"*

---

*All of which "relics of the servants of God" were preserved in Bunyan's *House Beautiful!*

than in any relic of the New Dispensation. Bunyan quotes
with enthusiasm from Moses and David, Job and Hezekiah;
his pilgrims press forward to meet Abraham, Isaac, and
Jacob; and at the gate of the Celestial City they meet not
Peter with his immemorial keys, but Enoch, Moses, and
Elijah!

Nor must it be supposed that our preacher's doctrinal sins
were confined to those of omission. He was excessively fond
of discoursing upon the "total depravity" of the natural man,
whose every imagination is evil and whose righteousness
shows but as filthy rags before God. And he was considered
a prime exponent of "justification by faith" — that theory in
which Good Will takes the place of Good Deeds, and Christ's
righteousness, instead of sanctifying *our* efforts, must be *im-
puted* to us and wrapped round us as a garment. From this
root sprang all those strange and somewhat hysterical details
of personal "conversion," or "acceptance" of Christ; the con-
viction of sin, the groaning and agony of spirit, the terror
lest God should not have predestined the soul to salvation,
and finally the self-assured revelation of sanctification and
grace. These things were everyday experiences among the
Puritans, recorded as authentically of Oliver Cromwell or of
Bunyan himself as of Hopeful or Christian. It was not a
cheerful philosophy of life; it admitted of no "indifferent"
actions, and it placed a rare premium upon scrupulosity.
Here, for instance, are some of John Bunyan's confessions of
the period just preceding his own conversion:

"Before this I had taken much delight in ringing, but now
I thought such practice vain, yet my mind hankered; wherefore I would go to the steeple-house and look on, though I
durst not ring. But I began to think: *How if one of the bells*

should fall? Then I chose to stand under a main beam that lay athwart the steeple, thinking here I might stand sure; but then I thought again, should the bell fall with a swing, it might first hit the wall and then rebounding, kill me. This made me stand in the steeple door; but then it came into my mind *How if the steeple itself should fall?* And this thought, as I looked on, did so shake my mind that I durst not stand at the steeple door any longer, but was forced to flee. . . ."

"Another thing was my dancing. I was full a year before I could leave that; but all this while, when I did anything that I thought was good, I had great peace with my conscience. But, poor wretch as I was, I was ignorant of Jesus Christ, and going about to establish my own righteousness. . . ."

One turns back with a sigh to the wholesome, unstudied sanity of pre-Reformation standards. Excesses of imagination there were indubitably throughout the great Middle Ages, and excesses of conduct, too; but the source of life was sound. And the England of Catholic discipline, of vigil and holy-day, was the only *merry* England the world has ever known. There is a little passage in *The World and the Child* — an interlude printed by Wynkyn de Worde in 1522 — quite wonderful in its balanced wisdom. The Child has long since grown to Manhood, with the scars of full many sins upon his soul, when upon a day Conscience comes to remonstrate. And Manhood cries out in that old and heart-sick query:

> What, Conscience, should I leave all game
> and glee?

> CONSCIENCE: Nay, Manhood, so mot I thee,
> All mirth in measure is good for thee:
> But, sir, measure is in all thing!

That was the perennial answer of the Catholic Church — a very great and very simple answer.

Now, in spite of its tendency to foster hypocrisy, there is no gainsaying the downright and terrible sincerity of the Puritan ideal. Bunyan spoke as the mouthpiece of a whole class of society — people of definite, even rigid piety, with a passion for "profitable discourses," for finely spun if perverse metaphysics, and a vigorous determination to tone down the rainbow pageantry of life to a pervasive and non-committal leaden grey. That was Christianity as they saw it; for they had forgotten the apostles and saints and martyrs, they knew not the Fathers, and the traditions of medievalism were anathema to them. On the other hand, we find the literature of the Old Faith for the most part exceedingly direct and elemental. *She* knew the heart of man, as her divine Founder had known, and needed not that any should tell her what was in man! And so the weakness and the potential heroisms of human nature were ever frankly in her thought. *Do penance and ye shall be saved* — that was the burden of the Church: her peremptory yet consoling message to a world in need alike of discipline and of solace! To quote once again from *The World and the Child:*

> Though a man had do alone
> The deadly sins everychone,
> And he with contrition make his moan
> To Christ our Heaven King,
> God is all so glad of him,
> As of the creature that never did sin. . . .

There, in truth, is a simple and authoritative evangelism: and the formula of repentance held out to Manhood (or Old Age, as he has now become) is equally free from morbidity or vagueness. He must "take him to abstinence," and keep in heart the Ten Commandments and the Twelve Articles of the Christian Creed. Verily, as Edgar Poe once said, "Truth is not always in a well. In fact, as regards the more important knowledge, I do believe that she is invariably superficial."

But the interlude we have been quoting cannot fail to remind the reader of an even finer and more familiar example — the moral play of *Everyman*. The allegory of this early Pilgrim was published some eight or ten years later than *The World and the Child,* but in method and in ideals it is thoroughly medieval. If (as a one-time editor has contended!) it was designed "to inculcate great reverence for old Mother Church and her Popish superstitions," it is the most vital and arresting apologetic in existence. It contains not one word of controversy, but a brief and highly dramatic allegory of man's summoning to death and judgment. Long ago the "most ingenious Dr. Percy" pointed out how "in this old simple drama the fable is conducted upon the strictest model of the Greek tragedy. The action is simply one, the time of action is that of the performance, the scene is never changed, nor the stage ever empty." The characters, too, are conceived in severest simplicity. They are abstractions as strict as any of Bunyan's, and yet, almost without exception, they are of a terrible and haunting reality. Those of us who have seen the morality well performed will need no reminder of this compelling humanity of the story; nor can those be unconscious of it who merely read the lines. First comes the brief yet noble address of Messenger, praying his audience to hear with reverence this moral play, "which of our lives and ending shows" — a matter wondrous precious, but with intent "more gracious and sweet to bear away."

The story saith: Man, in the beginning
Look well, and take good heed to the ending,
   Be you never so gay:
Ye think sin in the beginning full sweet,
Which in the end causeth thy soul to weep,
   When the body lieth in clay.
Here shall you see how Fellowship and Jollity,
Both Strength, Pleasure, and Beauty,
   Will fade from thee as flower in May;
For ye shall hear how our Heaven King
Calleth Everyman to a general reckoning:
   Give audience, and hear what he doth say. . . .

It is not merely the dramatic form, the superior condensation of plot, which place this allegory so many leagues above Bunyan's. To the average reader these might even seem an added difficulty: and the *raison d'être* of *Everyman* is frankly to edify. But its atmosphere is at once freer, more poignant, and more poetic: as different as the atmosphere of — say, medieval Oxford or Canterbury from that of Nonconformist Bedford!

Everyman himself is first seen walking blithely upon his way, his mind "on fleshly lusts and his treasure," and full little upon that dread messenger about to intercept him. Death's summons strikes confusion, then terror to his heart; and so the terse dialogue wears on:

EVERYMAN: Full unready I am such reckoning to give:
          I know thee not; what messenger art thou?

DEATH: I am death, that no man dreadeth;
          For everyman I 'rrest, and no man spareth.
          For it is God's commandment
          That all to me should be obedient.

In a sudden despairing hope the worldling essays to bribe his summoner, offering even a thousand pounds if he will defer this matter till another day. But Death sets no store by silver or gold, and tarries not for pope, king, or emperor; neither do Everyman's bitter tears avail him for a respite. The imperious one but reiterates his call to judgment, demanding a little scornfully:

> What, weenest thou thy life is given thee,
> And thy worldly goods also?

EVERYMAN: I had ween'd so verily.

DEATH: Nay, nay; it was but lend thee:
For, as soon as thou art gone,
Another awhile shall have it, and then go
therefro'
Even as thou hast done.
Everyman, thou art mad, thou hast thy
wits five,
And here on earth will not amend thy life;
For suddenly do I come.

Then follows Everyman's impassioned search for a companion in this pilgrimage, with the refusal of Fellowship, Kindred, and his worldly Goodes. It is only in a last desolation that he seeks out Good Deeds, where she lies prostrate beneath the burden of his own sins. But if she may not rise for weakness, Good Deeds has a healing counsel to give; she directs Everyman to her sister Knowledge, who in turn leads him on to Confession. And Shrift is not vainly sought, nor without comfort; he bestows upon Everyman a precious jewel, "called penance, voider of adversity," and likewise the scourge of Mortification. So in the name of the Holy Trinity, the pilgrim begins his strong penance; and ere long he weeps "for very sweetness of joy," as Good Deeds is seen arising to his aid. Knowledge has one more gift for Everyman — a tunic soaked in his own tears:

> It is the garment of sorrow,
> From pain it will you borrow;
> Contrition it is,
> That getteth forgiveness;
> It pleaseth God passing well.

When these bittersweet remedies have been wisely used, and Everyman passes out to receive the "Holy Sacrament and Ointment together," there is an interesting discourse between Knowledge and the Five Wits. It concerns the dignity and power of the priesthood; and while there are plain words for a few faithless shepherds, "blinded by sin," its substance is, briefly, that no emperor, king, duke, nor baron hath commission from God as hath the least priest in all the world —

> For of the blessed sacraments pure and benign
> He beareth the keys, and thereof hath cure
> For man's redemption, it is ever sure.

Everyman returns, pardoned at last, and the Death March is begun. A mortal faintness falls upon the pilgrim as he nears the grave; one after another Strength, Beauty, and Discretion forsake him, till only Knowledge and his Good Deeds remain. Then, crying out for mercy and commending his soul to God, Everyman suffers "that we shall all endure." But the angels' song is heard "making great joy and melody" as the freed soul is welcomed into its heavenly sphere: and the last solemn lesson of the tragic story is summed up by the Doctor's epilogue.

We have been speaking rather insistently about the direct
and practical simplicity of Catholic literature in those very
Catholic days — about its bearing upon the fundamental
facts of human life. That is one side of a great truth: but
there is another side. Religion is never merely utilitarian. Its
ultimate aim is not simply to make men virtuous, but to
bring the soul into eternal union with its God. And so the
simple merges and is lost in the sublime — the faith of stern,
immediate practicality is shown to be the mother of fair love
and of mysticism. The medieval temper, at once so fierce and
so inalienably poetic, understood this to a marvel. Through
the stress and struggle of a semibarbaric life it retained the
most intimate if ingenuous familiarity with heavenly things.
It seems almost a truism to reiterate all this in the face of
Dante and the Legend of the Grail; yet it is a fact rather too
little appreciated by the modern world. We may be reason-
ably certain that echoes of the miracle play and the old mystic
and romantic writings had sounded through John Bunyan's
youth. His own work was the richer for them; but it is poor,
indeed, beside them! It is poor first of all in ideas (though
not in fancy), and then it is poor in all the rarer gifts of
vision, of insight, and of ecstasy. The author of the *Pilgrim's
Progress* was preaching, for the most part, what generations
of his medieval precursors had been expounding: an allegory
of man hovering between two eternities. He merely, and inevitably, translated it into the terms of his own age and his
own people. It happened — for obvious reasons — that these
terms were less beautiful and less spacious than those of the
preceding time. These changed habits of thought are notice-
able not only in the innovations and omissions of the reform-
ers, but even in their attitude toward universally accepted

truths. Perhaps they may be gauged most significantly at the two poles of the spiritual life, Hell and Heaven.

Christian's entrance into the Celestial City has already been described, but from the Shining Men who lead him thither one may glean some further details. It is a perfectly orderly and conventional picture of Heaven. There the pilgrims will find Mount Sion, the tree of life, the innumerable company of angels, and the spirits of just men made perfect. They will see no more such things as they saw upon earth, "to wit, sorrow, sickness, affliction, and death, 'for the former things are passed away.'" And upon the men inquiring what they must do in this holy place, it is answered:

"You must there receive the comforts of all your toil, and have joy for all your sorrow; you must reap what you have sown, even the fruit of all your prayers and tears. . . . There you shall enjoy your friends again, that are gone thither before you . . . [and] be clothed with glory and majesty, and put into an equipage fit to ride out with the King of Glory. When He shall come with sound of trumpet in the clouds, as upon the wings of the wind, you shall come with Him; and when He shall sit upon the throne of judgment, you shall sit by Him; yea, and when He shall pass sentence upon the workers of iniquity . . . you also shall have a voice in that judgment."

A company of the heavenly host, and "several of the King's trumpeters, clothed in white and shining raiment," come out to welcome the pilgrims, so that with melodious noise they mount upward together. And "Oh," writes Bunyan in pious delight, "by what tongue or pen can their glorious joy be expressed?" The vision is touching in its simple sincerity; but once more one is forced to observe how much of its sublimity was owing to the Scriptures, and how crude or puerile the personal note tended to become.

Now we know that the Puritans thought a great deal about future punishment — both for themselves and for others — and we might expect from them a certain eloquence on the subject of Hell. Milton is no representative guide in the matter, since he stood apart and aloof in his ideals, dreaming his dreams as poet rather than as Puritan. So let us turn once again to Christian's experiences. It is when passing through the Valley of the Shadow of Death that Bunyan's Pilgrim comes upon the mouth of Hell. "And ever and anon the flame and smoke would come out in such abundance, with sparks and hideous noises (things that cared not for Christian's sword, as did Apollyon before) that he was forced to put up his sword and betake himself to another weapon called All-Prayer. . . . Also he heard doleful voices, and rushings to and fro, so that sometimes he thought he should be torn in pieces, or trodden down like mire in the streets."

Beyond reproach is Bunyan's "high seriousness," but his imagination will stretch no further. After all, he was but a poor descendant of that earlier John — a thirteenth-century churchman, and author of *The Soul's Ward.** In this old homily we meet perhaps the most astounding Inferno in English literature, and one of the few which can stand comparison with Dante's. Fear, the lean and pallid messenger of Death, visits the Soul's Castle for the better admonition of its keepers: and Prudence (who ever knoweth best how to beset her words and works) questions whence he cometh.

"'I come,' he saith, 'from Hell.' 'From Hell?' saith Prudence, 'and hast thou seen Hell?' 'Yea, truly,' saith Fear,

---

*Cf. *Old English Homilies.* Early English Text Society Publications, Vols. XXIX to XXXIV.

'often and frequently.' 'Now, then,' saith Prudence, 'upon thy troth tell us truly what Hell is like, and what thou hast seen therein.' 'And I will, blithly,' saith Fear, 'upon my troth; nevertheless, not according as it really is, for no tongue can tell that, but as far as I may and can I will discourse thereof. Hell is wide without measure, and deep and bottomless; full of incomparable fire, for no earthly fire may be compared therewith; full of stench intolerable, for no living thing on earth might endure it; full of unutterable sorrow, for no mouth may on account of the wretchedness and of the woe thereof, give an account of nor tell about it. Yea, the darkness therein is so thick that one may grasp it, for the fire there gives out no light, but blindeth the eyes of them that are there with a smothering smoke, the worst of smokes. And nevertheless in that same black darkness they see black things as Devils, that ever maul and afflict and harass them with all kinds of torture. . . . There is shrieking in the flame, and chattering of teeth in the snowy waters. Suddenly they flit from the heat into the cold, nor ever do they know of these two which is the worse for them, for each is intolerable. . . . And this same wanhope [*despair*] is their greatest torment, that none have never any more hope of any recovery, but are sure of every ill, to continue in woe, world without end, ever in eternity. Each chokes the other, and each hateth another and himself as the black Devil; and even as they loved them the more in this world, so the more shall they hate them there.' "

But not Fear himself, though he had a thousand tongues of steel, may fully recount the terrors of this abode of woe. " 'Now, Lord God!' quoth Prudence, 'guard and preserve us, and direct and advise us what we ought to do, and that we may be the more cautious and vigilant to keep ourselves safe on each side under God's wings. If we well guard and keep our house and God's dear treasure that He has intrusted to us, let death come whenever she will, we need not be in dread of her nor of Hell; for our death will be precious to God, and entrance into Heaven!'" There is the sweetness, the sanity again! The medieval imagination has been stretched to its farthest bounds of terror (which carries one well into the superlative degree!) and the fruit of it is a healthy recoil, an instantaneous prayer for God's grace — no morbid introspection, not a shade of spiritual hypochondria.

Even while speaking, Prudence beholds another messenger approach, "very glad in cheer, fair and joyful, and lovely attired." It is Love of Life, the herald of mirth and everlasting life, sent from the Blessed God lest His children be overmuch cast down by Fear. The soul's wards press about him right eagerly, praying that he tell them somewhat of God and His eternal bliss. But once again the infinite confounds human thought and utterance. Not as He is, declares Love of Life, may God be seen, for beside His brightness the sunbeam is dark and seemeth a shadow. Only for a little while and through a mirror which shielded his eyes has this messenger endured to gaze upon the Holy Trinity, three and indivisible. "But somewhat longer I was able to behold our Lord Jesus Christ, God's Son, that redeemed us on the cross — how He sits blissful on the right hand of His Father, who is almighty, and ruleth in that eternal life without cessation. So marvelous is His beauty that the angels are never satiated in beholding Him. And moreover I saw plainly the places of His wounds, and how He showeth them to His Father, to make known how He loved us, and how He was obedient to Him who sent Him thus to redeem us, and He beseecheth Him ever for mankind's heal. After Him I saw on high, above all heavenly hosts, the Blessed Virgin, His mother, called Mary, sitting on a throne so very bright, adorned with gems, and her face so joyful that every earthly light is darkness in comparison with it. . . . When I could no longer endure that light, I looked towards the angels and archangels and to the others that are above them, blessed spirits who are ever before God and ever serve Him, and sing ever unweariedly."

Of all the nine hierarchical hosts Love of Life next tells the beatitude; of the Apostles, "poor and low on earth," but now exalted above king or kaiser; of the holy martyrs and confessors; and of the consecrated virgins, whose presence yields so fair a perfume that "one might live ever by the sweetness." And then Prudence entreats him to explain somewhat that bliss which is common to all alike of the emparadised.

"They live ever in a splendor that is sevenfold brighter and clearer than the sun," answers the joyous messenger, "and ever in a strength to perform, without any toil, all that they wish, and evermore in a state, in all that ever is good, without diminution, without anything that may harm or ail, in all that is ever soft or sweet. And their life is the sight of God and the knowledge of God, as our Lord hath said. *That is eternal life,* He said, *to see and know the true God and Him that He hath sent, Jesus Christ our Lord.* . . . They are so wise that they know all God's counsels, His mysteries and His dooms. . . . They love God without measure . . . and each one loveth another as much as himself. So glad they are of God that all their bliss is so great that no mouth may make mention of it, nor any speech discourse of it. Because that each one loveth another as himself, each one hath of another's bliss as much joy as of his own. . . . Take heed now then, if the heart of no one is ever able to contain in herself her own special joy, so marvelously great is the one bliss, how shall she accept so many and so great blisses? Therefore our Lord said to those that had pleased Him: *Intra in gaudium Domini tui — Go,* quoth He, *into thy Lord's bliss.* Thou must go therein altogether and be altogether possessed therein, for in thee may it in nowise enter. . . ." *The Soul's Ward* is a precious random jewel from the rich coffers of medieval lore, as notable for its refinement of thought and mystical insight as for its very colorful and vigorous imagination. Right gladly must we all comply with the pious request which brings the old homily to a close, and, *"par seinte charité,* pray a *pater noster* for John who wrote this book."

To what may one attribute the innate wisdom which stretched from end to end mightily and ordered all things so sweetly throughout this religious literature of the Middle Ages? I think we must say, to the saints. The Church in every era *teaches* truth: but these children of her heart *live* the truth. They irradiate the *beauty of holiness,* and create a spiritual intuition which only centuries of unbelief can quite eradicate. In spite of much evil, a society which produces saints — or to whom God vouchsafes these miracles of His grace — must be at bottom a faithful society. And again, the people among whom saints move (although possibly they may stone them!) will assuredly be unable to forget their influence. All the Christian ideals of conduct have been clinched and verified by the saints — those *geniuses in sanctity,* as Francis Thompson has called them. Walter Pater somewhere speaks of Catherine of Siena as transcending "not by her rectitude of soul only, but by its fairness." That is a most significant tribute. For Puritanism, too, had its share in rectitude of soul: it was the ideal set before us with much earnestness and no little genius throughout the *Pilgrim's Progress*. But — fairness? The old sweet intimacy with spiritual things, fruit alike of meditation and the sacraments, had faded from Bunyan's horizon. The old authoritative interpretation, and not less the old fervent and unconscious poetry, were fast fading. How much they meant, to art as well as to life, we find by opening the pages of these old Catholic allegories. They were written for frail people, for sinful people — that is to say, for people very like ourselves. They had many a quaint and curious turn of national *patois*. But they spoke the language of the saints. That, like the Pentecostal tongue, is at root the language understood by every nation under heaven. It is the language of high poetry, too: and somehow, even from the beginning, it has proved itself the sole medium for transmuting a wistful yet reluctant world.

JEANNE D'ARC
THE SUNSET OF THE MIDDLE AGES—
THE DAWN OF MODERNITY

O N TWELFTH Night, the Feast of the Magi, in the
year 1412, Jeanne d'Arc was born in the little Lorraine village of Domrémy. All the world knows, or mis-
knows, her story; for while she and the Poverello of Assisi
stand at opposite poles of sainthood, they have at least this
in common, that they continue down the centuries to attract
every possible variety of biographer. The just and the unjust
have fought over Jeanne's faithful ashes — the German poet,
the American humorist, the agnostic French philosopher, the
paradoxical Irish dramatist have, each in his own way, contributed to her compelling immortality. And our own century has seen the final reparation for one of the greatest
crimes in history: Jeanne looks down today not only from the
walls of the Pantheon but from the altars of the Catholic
Church.

There was never a cult more salutary than this cult of *La
Pucelle* — never a canonization more timely in our professedly feminist and profoundly hazardous age. The curious
fact is that Jeanne d'Arc should not be more confidently
claimed, more universally exploited by women themselves,
both within and without the Church; since there is scarcely
in all history a figure who embodies in so quintessential a

degree the ideals toward which modern womanhood is striving. We all remember the Westminster epitaph of Margaret, Duchess of Newcastle, for whose family it was proudly claimed that "all the brothers were valiant and all the sisters virtuous." But the goal of the modern woman, at its soundest and sanest and sweetest, is both higher and more inclusive — it would have the sisters valiant as well as virtuous, the brothers virtuous as well as valiant.

This is precisely the ideal which Jeanne d'Arc so simply and whole-heartedly fulfilled. Obviously she was a *specialist* in all her public career. The work which, for particular national reasons, she was called to do lay distinctly outside the normal province of womanhood — the way she did it, as distinctly within. Indeed, it is rather important to remember that there is nothing in life or art, nothing great or humble, nothing from darning socks to writing sonnets, which would not become more beautiful, more effectual, if done in that spirit of largeness and singleness and consecration which she embodied! Through the records of her Trial and Rehabilitation* a thousand intimate personal characteristics flame out like golden banners. Concerning the childhood and girlhood when she was growing up in war-torn Domrémy — used to the more or less hopeless tales of English victory and French defeat, used also to the necessity of occasional flight with her family from predatory bands of soldiers, yet learning to sew and spin and watch the flocks, as became the daughter of a prosperous peasant farmer — we have a few charming but perfectly normal anecdotes. There is, for instance, the story of

*See, for the most complete Englishing of Quicherat's monumental translation of the original documents into modern French: *The Trial of Jeanne d'Arc*, translated by W. P. Barrett (Gotham House, Inc.) and *Jeanne d'Arc, Maid of Orleans, Deliverer of France*, edited by T. Douglas Murray (Heinemann and McClure, Phillips & Co.).

the neighboring verger whom Jeanne bribed by little presents of wool to work more diligently in his belfry: he had known all her brief life in the village, and testified to her grave and gentle modesty, her devotion to the offices of the Church, her helpfulness to the poor, and her industry, whether at the loom, the plow or the pasture. Then come the artless depositions of the women of Domrémy, who used to walk to and from Mass with "Jeannette"; who remembered her kneeling in the fields when the church bells rang, or dancing with the other village maidens, or bringing nuts and provisions for the annual picnic at the Ladies' Tree on Laetare Sunday. "I did not know of Jeanne's departure," cried one of these women tristfully after the lapse of quarter of a century: "I wept much — I loved her dearly for her goodness and because she was my friend."

From quite another angle comes the testimony of those who knew the Maid during her fifteen months of militant service. The Sieur de Metz saw Jeanne first when she traveled up to Vaucouleurs in her shabby frock of red serge, pleading with Robert de Baudricourt for the third time for soldiers to lead her to the young dauphin at Chinon. She had been twice refused, and she never argued the subject; she simply returned to the attack. But the fire of unquenchable purpose was burning beneath this maidenly calm, and it blazed up when the knight inquired with mild curiosity when she wished to start. "Better at once than tomorrow," came the characteristic retort, "and better tomorrow than later!" That was at the very beginning of her public career — she scarcely knew as yet how to balance a lance on horseback. But when her poor, dazed sovereign was celebrating the mighty victory she had won for him at Orléans, and making the peasant-maid *grande chère,* the identical spirit answered him: "Noble

Dauphin, hold not such long and so many councils, but start at once for Rheims and there receive your crown."

Jeanne's swiftness of thought and directness of action were a constant marvel to the men about her — men who too well remembered Agincourt, and had ceased even to hope aggressively. Probably they were also very much confused about the real rights of the French succession. There is a sense in which Bernard Shaw was correct enough in his contention that Jeanne d'Arc was the *first nationalist;* for almost alone of her century she seems to have perceived that the old feudal order was definitely passed, that the nations of Europe had become separate entities, and that each country belonged to the people living in it and to their own legitimate rulers. How she attained this sweeping vision is one of the amazing questions of her amazing life, for an unlettered girl can scarcely have worked out the matter philosophically. But either by the intuition of genius or the direct revelation of sainthood, she knew when a page of history had been turned. "Get back to *your own country,* God with you," she dictated in the first of those astounding letters addressed to the English regent, Bedford; "and if this is not done expect news of the Maid, who will shortly go to see you to your very great damage." Her going was to besieged Orléans in that May of 1430, where after two days of fighting she and her troops were completely victorious. It was the "sign" or seal of her divine mission which she had promised the doubting dauphin. . . . And being, during her trial two years later, hypocritically questioned about inciting her king to "shed human blood," she cited her efforts to negotiate peace with the neighboring duke of Burgundy, but insisted: "As for the English, the only peace with them is by their return to their own country, *to England.*"

One little incident before the attack upon Jargeau reveals the winsomeness as well as the force of the mighty Maid. "Forward, gentle duke, to the assault!" she cried, bursting in upon his grace of Alençon about nine o'clock one morning. He protested that the assault was premature, and pleaded for delay; whereupon Jeanne, with that high queenliness of hers, gave the superb answer: "It is the right time when it pleases God, we must work when it is His will. *Travaillez, et Dieu travaillera!*" Yet never a prophet was gentler to the weakness of the flesh. "Ah, gentle duke," she said, turning back when she saw that her point was gained, "dost thou not know that I promised thy wife to bring thee back whole and sound?"

No one seems to have studied Jeanne more intelligently or more sympathetically during all this time than her *"beau duc,"* as she used to call him. D'Alençon was a prince of the blood royal, commander-in-chief, until her own coming, of the French armies, and his testimony is full of significance. He was hunting quails at St. Florent — having recently been ransomed at enormous price from a three-year imprisonment by the English — when news was brought of the young peasant girl who had come to Charles VII with the dizzying message that God had sent her to raise the siege of Orléans and drive the English out of France. Not unnaturally, the duke made his own way right speedily to the impoverished little court at Chinon — and his capitulation was immediate. Seeing, he believed; or it may be that believing, he saw. . . . Side by side they followed the weary marches, the daring, glorious engagements of her campaign of the Loire. It is not certain where d'Alençon was when the Maid was captured by the Burgundians at Compiègne and later sold to the English, or while the grim tragedy of her trial was being played to its end. But some twenty-five years later, when by order of Pope Calixtus III the doctors assembled in Notre Dame to inquire into the validity of the Rouen sentence, the duke came up to Paris to give his testimony. The picture of Jeanne's white fire of purity, her hatred of blasphemy and of the evil women who followed the camp, her tact in dealing with the various generals, her reverent piety, came upon him then in a wave of impassioned memory. "I think truly, it was God who led us," he declared of her brief generalship; and the sum of his deposition fell into these momentous words:

"I always held her for an excellent Catholic and a modest woman; she communicated often, and at sight of the Body of Christ, shed many tears. In all she did, except in affairs of war, she was a very simple young girl; but in warlike things — bearing the lance, assembling an army, ordering military operations . . . she was most skillful. Everyone wondered that she should act with as much wisdom and foresight as a captain who had fought for twenty or thirty years. It was above all in making use of artillery that she was so wonderful."

Of course, d'Alençon erred in this last sentence. The wonder of Jeanne d'Arc was never more preëminent than when she faced her court of accusers (it cannot be said that the tribunal boasted any judges!) in the English citadel at Rouen. To martyrdom she marched valiantly enough in all truth, but each step of the way was fought soldier-wise. Every power on earth was marshaled against the girl: learning and treachery and might and brutality and — hardest of all to bear — the *appearance* of righteous authority. For these men, whom Jeanne knew to be fighting God, fought ostensibly in God's name! That was the consummate irony of it all. Bed-

ford, the capable English regent, and his colleague of Win-
chester, were not content merely to imprison or to kill the
Maid: they determined to impugn her entire work. They
wished to place the ban of sacrilege and illegitimacy upon
her king's coronation at Rheims. Hence it was decreed to try
Jeanne for heresy and witchcraft — a wave of this latter
phobia having, according to Pierre Champion,* reached its
sinister high-water mark in fifteenth-century Europe — before a tribunal of English sympathizers carefully suborned
for the end in view. She seems to have taken no great trouble
to conceal her scorn of them, and answered with so high a
spirit that one of Henry's own soldiers was heard to exclaim:
"This is a brave woman. Would she were English!" Without
legal counsel, day after day and week after week, she faced
her inquisitors with the same patient fire. From the first she
had refused to take oath save upon matters bearing directly
upon her case; and when urged to violate this "precept of
silence" in matters concerning her king or her Voices, the
only answer was a proudly determined *Passez-outre* — or a
humbly determined *I refer me to our Lord*. Again and yet
again, Jeanne's simplicity triumphed over the most abstruse
and subtly framed interrogations; as when, being asked
whether she was certain of being in God's grace, she gave the
immortal answer: "If I am not, may God put me there —
if I am, may God so keep me." And finally, at a hint from
the friendly Brother Isambard, she shattered the validity of
the whole trial by appealing her cause directly to the Pope
and the Council of Bâle. It was a master-stroke, had Cauchon
retained decency enough to hold to any appearance of justice.
But he drowned her voice with a cry of "Hold your tongue

*See *The Trial of Jeanne d'Arc, ut supra.*

in the devil's name!" and ordered the appeal stricken off the minutes of the notary. Had he not repeated letters from the University of Paris expressing impatience at the length of the trial — and one from "Henry, by the grace of God, king of France and England" (aged at that time ten years!), declaring: "It is our intention to retake and regain possession of this Jeanne, if it comes to pass that she is not convicted or found guilty — "? For an ambitious and utterly unscrupulous man, the stakes were really too high!

Jeanne's largeness of vision (another side, after all, to her simplicity) might well have shamed the triviality of her hunters. "My Lord has a book in which no clerk has ever read, how perfect soever he be in clerkship," she had answered sagely when the populace cried out that never had deeds like hers been read of anywhere. And now she made brief work of the questions about St. Michael's hair, or the clothing worn by St. Catherine or St. Margaret. When taunted with neglecting the work proper to womankind, in order to save France from English invasion, she replied with beautiful and unanswerable logic: "There are plenty of other women to do *that!*" So, too, with the interminable questions about her male attire. It would seem fairly obvious that, having a man's work to do, and living among men in the rough camp and rougher prison, Jeanne's chosen dress was the only safe or sensible one for her to assume. But the Rouen judges affected to find in it one of their chiefest scandals, and it held conspicuous place in the formal bill of accusation eventually brought against the hapless Maid. She denied repeatedly that any other human being should be held responsible for this "dissolute" attire, and explained as best she could that she believed it, under the circumstances, not only indifferent but even positively pleasing to Almighty God. Then, when her explanations were met by added obliquity of questioning, she dismissed the subject with one perfect sentence: "What con-, cerns this dress is a small thing — less than nothing." One would give much to have seen Jeanne's eyes when she spoke those words!

To be sure, they broke her spirit in the end. After the trial had lasted five months, when his prisoner's mind and body were manifestly forespent by the long days of inquisition and the nights of abuse and insult, it occurred to Pierre Cauchon to have the girl publicly exhorted in the cemetery of St. Ouen. So, in the presence of her lordly accusers and of the "good people" of Rouen, she was led out upon a scaffold or gallery to be harangued with many accusations by one Maître Guillaume Erard. The executioner, and a stake already prepared with faggots, were facing her. Then did Jeanne d'Arc commit the one great crime, the one great frailty of her stainless life: for a frenzied moment she ceased to believe in herself! It was true — all that they witnessed. against her — she had been deluded. But the guilt was upon her own shoulders, not her King's! And she begged the judges to take her away from the fire — of which she had peculiar dread — and place her in the prisons of the Church, with women to care for her. . . . There is not, in all the tear-stained records of human tragedy, an incident of more poignant pathos than this recantation of the Maid of Orleans. It occurred just one year and a day after her capture outside the drawbridge of Compiègne, and when the girl was a few months past her nineteenth birthday.

That was the first and last surrender. Four days later came the glorious "relapse" which brought Jeanne so quickly to the stake. Cauchon hastened to the castle prison — where, against his sworn word, he had returned the prisoner after her submission — and found her clothed again in her right mind, and in her male attire. There was no wavering in her *Credo* this time. "If I said that God had not sent me, I should damn myself, for it is true that God has sent me," she told the bishop vehemently. "All that I said and revoked, I said for fear of the fire . . . I did not intend so to do or to say, I did not intend to deny my visions." It was Jeanne of Orléans, of Patay, of Rheims, speaking then; the Jeannette of Dom-rémy, too, as with sweet but firm *naïveté* she recounted how her saints had told of the great sorrow they felt for the treason into which she had been led — to deny and abjure her deeds in order to save her life. . . . Within two days came the "deliverance" which these Voices had so often yet so cryptically prophesied, and which the Martyr-Maid had, for awhile, but ill understood. On the thirtieth day of May, in the year 1431, calling to the last upon the name of Jesus, Jeanne d'Arc climbed the ladder of flames from France to God.

The matter of these Voices cannot any longer be begged, since upon their authenticity the Maid of France quite literal-ly staked her life. She left her home to lead the French armies to victory and the French King to his crown — and in the end went to the stake rather than abjure her mission — for the single reason that she believed herself a sword chosen and wielded by the hand of God. And she believed this because, as she herself declared, she had been so told, so commanded, by "her brothers in Paradise." There is small strangeness, of course, to the Catholic mind, in this more personal and intimate manifestation of the mysterious Com-munion of Saints. The vessel of election in every age has been wrought for service — or it may be, merely guided toward the way of service — by hands other than material. And although Jeanne was rather a silent woman, always given to deeds rather than words, her testimony about the Voices, first during the dauphin's inquiry at Chinon, and later during the endless, hostile interrogations of the Rouen trial, was full enough to be quite intelligible. The first Voice spoke to her at Domrémy one summer afternoon when she was but thirteen — suitably enough, it was the heavenly warrior, Michael — saying simply: "Be good — go often to church." With the words came a light, and the young girl, standing alone in her father's homely garden, feared at first; but it was not Jeanne's way to fear anything very long, least of all an angel. . . . A little later on came the apparitions of St. Catherine and St. Margaret, while the messages became at once more definite and more incredible: she — Jeanne — must go over from Lorraine into France — she must relieve the siege of Orléans — she must lead her dauphin to the anointing and coronation of his Kingship! For five years she kept these persistent words in her heart, telling the visions neither to her family nor even to her confessor. Then she simply but deliberately set about accomplishing the impossible.

During the first year of her military leadership, Jeanne seems to have been confirmed almost constantly by her saints. "You have been to your counsel," she said to the dissenting generals when they were trying — as usual — to hold her back from action, "and I have been to *mine,* and the counsel of God shall be accomplished." After the coronation at Rheims she acted more or less on her own authority: her divine commission was fulfilled. And it was then that she met, together with splendid victories, her first real defeats. But she was able to prophesy within some three weeks the date of her capture at Compiègne, and in prison she was not abandoned. On one occasion the Voice woke her as she "slept for sorrow" in the Rouen cell.

"Was it by touching you on the arm?" inquired her inquisitors somewhat fatuously.

"It woke me without touching," Jeanne answered: and then, with heart-shaking simplicity, she rehearsed the exquisite little drama of consolation. No, she did not fall upon her knees, but she thanked the visitant for coming. "I was sitting on the cot; I joined my hands; I implored its help. The Voice said to me: 'Answer them boldly. God will help thee!'"

So now we come close to the most fundamental point of all — the *source* of Jeanne's visions. The Rouen judges declared that these apparitions proceeded from the devil, and they dealt with her accordingly. M. Anatole France and his school declared they came from her own noble but unsound imagination, and *they* dealt with her accordingly. But the Maid herself said they came from God: and after one momentary weakness of denial, she sealed her faith with blood and with fire. So the mind of the Church, believing Jeanne and judging her inspiration by its fruits, has after five hundred years so dealt as to place the crown of sainthood upon her head. . . . Now it does not seem that Jeanne was particularly introspective or at all analytical. She did not question, as our modern ages question, the *how* and the *why* of Almighty God. But she listened, as few have listened in this garrulous world — then with an *Ecce ancilla Domini,* she threw herself unreservedly into the work of His will. And just this "one rapture of an inspiration" was the basic need of her disheartened people. Only a miracle could have raised fifteenth-century France to any belief in its own desperate cause, and the miracle was — "Jeannette!" By the dynamic force of her own divine and vivid certainty she lifted up the hearts of men. It was not simply her genius which ended the Hundred Years' War and saved the nationhood of France. It was not even her sanctity. It was the supreme, God-given belief in her own mission. And modern psychology has made it at least a little easier to understand that this belief is the one universal secret of hero and of saint.

But Jeanne's methods were all rational enough. Her angelic accolade brought no immunity from the daily lot of toil and pain. Like many another mystic, she was enormously efficient — and she knew only too well that she fought with armies of men, not of angels. She was the *practical idealist:* and that is why she was, at the beginning of this paper, suggested as so intimately significant to the woman of today, rather than because she raised the siege of Orléans or baffled the University of Paris. Almost unique in history was this peasant girl's *balance* of action and vision, of pride and humility, of strength and tenderness. She loved, indeed, to help bridge a moat or build a rampart; but she loved better still to kneel beside some dying French — or English — soldier. She used to say that she loved her banner forty times better than her sword! And best of all she loved to receive Holy Communion on the days when little children were allowed to bear her company to the church. For Jeanne walked not only by faith, but by what Coventry Patmore has pregnantly named the *corollaries* of faith. She believed largely — she gave all. And oftener than not, these corollaries are very human in expression. Love, as we know upon the highest authority, is translated by deed and by truth into obedience; and the whole counsels of perfection may underlie so simple a matter as walking up instead of down the street. It is all a matter of motive, of intention. The hero does great things: he may apparently do more than the saint. The difference is that the saint does great things for God! And then, fortunately for us, it is never possible, even in the highest and most potent life, to separate the universal from the personal. One of the personal characteristics of Jeanne d'Arc was her immense capacity for good work. She left much to God, but nothing to chance. Above this, she possessed three of the noblest virtues known to manhood or to womanhood: courage, simplicity, and the love of truth. They are none too common — in fact, they are rarer than most of us care to admit — but in them lies the hope of the race. And without them heroic sanctity, at least, is inconceivable. For courage is the belief in God and in self, a free and large virtue, the daughter of hope and the mother of action. And simplicity is the grace of shooting straight, without détour or distraction or self-consciousness; in one sense it may be called divine concentration. While to love truth, and to serve truth, with a passion absorbing life and death alike, is not far from the Kingdom of Heaven.

No virtue, and no vice, is confined to any single century. But in a sense almost symbolic, Jeanne summed up the particular virtues of medievalism — its absolute and beautiful faith, its quixotically self-sacrificing devotion to a cause, its enormous, youthful energy and vitality in action: just as her persecutors summed up the medieval vices of cruelty, superstition, oversubtlety and rapacity. In more ways than one, her passing marked the sunset of the Middle Ages — the dawn of Modernity. A little boy of Rouen, standing in the crowd before that awesome conflagration, would have witnessed in his manhood the final expulsion of the English from his country — *and* the invention of printing! He might easily have lived on to see the birth of those two typical Renaissance gentlemen, absolute egoists and absolute monarchs, Francis I of France and Henry VIII of England. Before he died, Martin Luther — champion of the religious revolt which had so long been rumbling throughout Europe — would have been born in Germany; while Spain would be rejoicing in the fall of the Moorish empire and the discovery of the New World.